Nancy Mericol

II Corinthians 1:3&4

This book is dedicated in loving memory to my parents

Frank James Miller, Senior
Born June 12, 1914
Disappeared October 8, 2000
Body Discovered April 19, 2001
Interred April 27, 2001

Louise Mae Nickell Miller
Born March 13, 1920
Departed This Life February 24, 2001
Interred February 28, 2001

ISBN 0-7414-1201-2

Published by:

PUBLISHING.COM

519 West Lancaster Avenue
Haverford, PA 19041-1413
Info@buybooksontheweb.com
www.buybooksontheweb.com
Toll-free (877) BUY BOOK
Local Phone (610) 520-2500
Fax (610) 519-0261

Printed in the United States of America

Printed on Recycled Paper

Published August, 2002

PROLOGUE

When I began writing "Down Life's Path" for The Jackson Herald, a weekly newspaper published in Ripley, West Virginia, I told Editor Mike Ruben I wanted my columns to hold a little humor, reflect nature, and inspire. I never dreamed that, within five months of that first June 2000 printing, humor would be the farthest thing from my mind, the meaning of nature would change for me forever, and writing my essays would become heartache for a time.

After October 8th, 2000, I wrote to keep readers informed of facts surrounding a personal tragedy. My eighty-six-year-old father, an Alzheimer's patient, wandered away from home that bitterly cold night. It seemed the earth swallowed him up. My grieving mother died unexpectedly and alone, in her back yard, on February 24th, 2001. Away from home, I wasn't aware of her death until two days later. My father's body was discovered on April 19th of that same year. Again, as with Mom, I was away from home at the time.

A friend called one night, during the early days of my trial, to console me. "Nancy," she said, "I can't wait to read a book you've written about your experience." Horrified, I replied, "I could never do that!"

But one night, after my father's funeral, the story began to form in my mind. I wrote several pages before stopping. I hope to someday finish and publish the memoir of this episode in my life, as a tribute to my beloved parents. But for now, this little book containing previously written columns, poems, and stories, accompanied with photos, will have to do. My pain is too fresh for more.

TIME MARCHES ON

On an early autumn morning, less than a month after my father's disappearance, I walked ahead of my husband, Jack, along a graveled road above our Monroe County camp. A miniature gold-and-lime maple leaf fell. Swirling gently down from a tree by the roadside, it came to rest at my feet.

As I walked on, the earth continued to turn slowly on its axis, and the sun continued to shine. It seemed only God and I were aware of the fallen leaf. Dad came to mind. I wrote the first two stanzas of the following poem. On May 4th 2001, nearly three months after Mom's death and two weeks after the discovery of Dad's body, I wrote the remaining stanzas.

Dew drips from a leaf, reminding me of tears shed for Dad

TWO FALLEN LEAVES

One leaf fell. Time walked on,
Unaware one leaf was gone.
The sun still arose, the tree still grew,
Leaves unfurling in the morning dew.
Unmindful of this one leaf that fell,
The earth spun on like a carousel.

One leaf fallen from our family tree,
Suspending the passing of time for me.
That one leaf lay in the morning dew,
But where it lay, God only knew.
That October night, as this one leaf fell,
The earth spun on like a carousel.

Trees wept in the October sun,
Leaves falling and covering the one,
Camouflaging it where it lay.
Time marched on from day into day.
Unmindful of the one leaf that fell,
The earth spun on like a carousel.

From autumn into spring, time marched on,
Our hearts still grieving for this leaf long gone.
Then one day, where we could not see,
Another leaf fell from our family tree.
We now grieved two leaves that fell
While the earth spun on like a carousel.

Then one April day, a man walked by;
In the fallen leaves, something caught his eye.
As new leaves unfurled and the tree still grew,
The first leaf was found in the morning dew.
Time walks on since those two leaves fell,
And the earth spins on like a carousel.

A FIERY BEGINNING

Mom told me many stories on our nature walks while on vacation. How thankful I am that Jack suggested early in our marriage that we take my parents with us as often as feasible, in spite of my reluctance at first to do so. The following story is an incident that happened soon after my birth.

Fire!

The chicken house was on fire! A gusty wind drove the flames against the little nearby farmhouse. An exhausted young man stood in the front yard of his home, two empty buckets hanging from limp hands. His shoulders sagged and sweat soaked his clothing, dripped from his black hair, and rolled down his face.

His breathing ragged, he gasped, "It's no use, Louise. I can't fight it." His wife, barely out of her teens, stood near him, two small children crying and clutching the hem of her skirt. She had stood protecting her babies and watching her husband's trips back and forth from the hand-dug well to their endangered home — useless trips, fighting a battle he couldn't win. The water thrown on the front of the blistering house hissed into steam before it hardly left the buckets.

"You'd better get the baby," the man said. "The house is going to burn." Disengaging herself from the toddlers' grip, the mother tore out around the house toward the back door. How could she forget the baby? Fear over the fire must have addled her.

The temperature inside the house shocked her. It was an inferno. The baby lay on its face in the crib, face screwed in anguish, newborn wails covered by the roar of the wind and raging fire. Snatching up the baby, the woman rushed back outside to her husband and her little ones.

3

Her heart ached with despair. What would they do without their home? There was no money, nowhere to go, except to crowd in with her parents, who still had four children at home in a two-bedroom house. This house they now lived in belonged to her husband's widowed mother.

"If only the wind would stop," her husband said. "Maybe then I'd have a chance." But the wind continued, driving the flames horizontally and mercilessly against their little home. The paint was oozing, the boards singed.

"Stop the wind, God!" Frank heard his wife yell. He looked up, startled. She stood, the baby tucked under her elbow, the arms of the two little ones wrapped around her knees. Her other arm pointed straight toward the burning chicken house. She stood strong and erect, confident in a God who had never failed them yet.

Do we really serve a God who can do that? Frank wondered. He didn't wonder long. No sooner had the words left his wife's lips than the wind ceased, changed directions and began blowing the opposite direction, the force strong enough to shoot the flames horizontally across the ground, never veering to right or left.

The wind didn't let up until the chicken house was in ashes. During that time, not once again did it blow toward the farm house, but kept its reversed direction, sweeping the hazardous flames away from the humble little home.

Do we really serve a God who can do that? Frank had asked. We certainly do. I was that baby tucked under my mother's arms while she called on a God she knew would not fail her. And He didn't. And neither has He failed me.

I don't always stand erect and certain, like my mother stood that long ago day. Sometimes I fall on my face and cry out in despair, begging as the searing heat of affliction

4

surrounds me. God does not forget me, as my mother did. He hears my cry and runs to pick me up and rescue me from the fiery heat of my trial.

I am not always secure in my prayers, as my mother was that day. Sometimes flames of doubt blow my way, threatening to incinerate my faith, but still I pray. I cry and clutch the hem of my Father's garment. He hears, holds me close, and comforts me.

Sometimes, like my earthly father, I try to do it on my own, and I fail. Sometimes, like him, I ask, *Do we really serve a God who can do that?* And the answer is always, yes, Yes, YES! He can, He will, and He does. My spiritual house stands, unbeaten by the flames of adversity, their merciless searing tongues doused by prayer — prayer offered up from a deep well of trust, inherited from my praying mother.

Printed in *The Sunday Digest,* January 15, 1994

TIME FOR A CHANGE

When I was about five, Mom and Dad bought a grocery store on Sugar Creek Drive, just outside of Charleston, West Virginia. Memories of Mom then are happy ones. I think it was good for her to get out of the house. In those days, she whistled while she worked.

Mother Whistler

Behind the candy counter,
She greeted customers
And counted out change.
She dusted and stocked sagging shelves,
Wrote out wholesale orders,
And tallied credit accounts,
Knowing some would be gratuitous,
Most slow in coming.
On an oiled, hand-cranked slicer,
She cut thick circles of red bologna
And squares of chopped ham and cheese,
Binding them in bulky sheets of
Brown paper secured with string.
Between customers, she
Crocheted lace doilies, embroidered pillowcases,
And appliqued quilts for the Ladies' Aide.
The fourth baby, nursed between customers,
Cozied in a crib by the ice cream freezer,
Lulled to sleep by the laboring motor until
A sudden slam of the screen door announced,
"Naptime's over!"

Mother Whistler (continued)

Evenings, Mom cooked and cleaned
For a family of six
While we children packaged change,
Counting to the jingle of coins
Weighty in our hands,
Reveling as the pyramid of rolls rose,
Not realizing, as she did,
The scarcity of dollars,
Or that the stack of bills and credit slips
Piled higher than paid receipts.
Late nights, she strung pole beans and
Hulled peas,
Hard little green pellets
Pinging into an aged aluminum dishpan.
Summers, when sweltering sun
Stole his desire for fishing,
Dad minded the store
While Mom picked berries,
Washing and selling them by the gallons.
In later years, I caught myself wondering
When she slept, how she kept smiling
Or why, in spite of everything,
She whistled a merry tune while she worked.

FIRE and WATER

It seems history, albeit rewritten, repeats itself. As fire endangered my life, flood would endanger the life of my infant. The dishpan mentioned above would figure in her salvation. Mom didn't have to tell me the following story. Living it, I will never forget the horror of that tragic, historic July day in 1961.

Flash Flood!

A loud, unidentified noise woke me in the middle of the night. I jerked up in bed, still weak from giving birth to my second child, a little girl named Kimberly. My heart pounded in fright. Reaching over, I touched my firstborn, who slept between my husband and me in the spare bed at my parents' home. Finding Jackie's breathing deep and even, I scrambled from bed, rushing to the bassinet to assure myself that my newborn infant also slept safely.

Kimberly was fine. But what was responsible for the terrifying, deafening roar? A light flicked on in the living room. My mother hurried to the bassinet, her eyes wide and a puzzled frown on her face. "Is she all right?" she asked.

Nodding my head, I questioned, "Mom, what's that terrible noise?"

"I think it's rain," she answered. "A cloudburst." She ran to the door and stepped out on the porch. "Frank! Frank!" she yelled, rushing back through the house toward her bedroom. "It's flooding. The water's rising fast. We'll have to get out."

I hurried to the porch, peering through the blinding rain, alarmed to find the small creek, normally shallow and placid, a raging, tumbling force carrying tires, garbage cans, and other debris along in its wake. The rain fell in heavy, silver sheets, beating against the tin roof in a continuous roar, covering the sound of the booming, racing waters.

The flood rose steadily, swirling over the yard toward the house. I froze as I saw my brother's car, usually parked by the creek, floating by, tossing like jetsam in the muddy stream, its wheels pointing toward the sky. I was thankful Bub lived high on the hill above us.

My parents raced from the bedroom, dressed and carrying umbrellas. My two younger sisters followed behind, rubbing sleep from their eyes. "Hurry, Nancy!" my mother called above the roar. "Wake up Jack and tell him to get Jackie. I'll take the baby. Frank, you help the girls and Nancy up the hill."

My father, who had stepped out in the crashing rain, came back inside, the umbrella in his hands collapsed and bent. "Louise," he said, "it's coming down like buckets. The umbrella's no good." Water streamed from him and pooled in the floor at his feet.

"Then we'll wrap the baby in a blanket," Mom said, picking Kimberly up from the bassinet.

"No! You can't!" I cried. "It won't work. It's raining too hard. The blanket will get soaked in that downpour, and Kimberly will smother or drown."

I began crying hysterically. My husband, Jack, awakened by the tumult, came from the bedroom and wrapped me in his arms. "Our babies will die!" I told him, tears running down my face.

"Now, Nancy," my mother spoke firmly, "stop that! We'll think of something." She paced back and forth, her brow creased in thought. "Frank," she spoke decisively to my father, "take the girls and Nancy on up the hill to the neighbors above us. Jack and I will bring the baby."

I'd witnessed my mother's stubborn resourcefulness for nineteen years. All I could do was trust my baby to her and my strong, caring husband — and pray. The deluge pouring over my head and down my face as I walked off the porch took my breath away. I prayed harder. If we could barely breathe, how would my fragile infant survive in this watery destruction?

We clawed our way up the steep hill, my father helping Jackie and me, my sisters shoved along by two neighbors who had joined us in our rush to safety. I could make out the dark shapes of other neighbors around us and hear the frightened cries of children, the heartbreaking sobbing of some of the women, and cursing of a few men. Several inches of rolling water washed over our feet and down the hill, adding to the fury of the burgeoning creek.

We finally reached the neighbor's house above us, where we joined over thirty people from the valley below seeking refuge from the storm. I refused to go inside, anxiously pacing the porch and praying earnestly.

At last the shadowy forms of my mother and husband broke through the dark storm. Jack shoved my plump mother up the hill from behind, while she held our precious newborn, wrapped in a warm blanket, in one arm. In her other hand, she held, inverted directly over the baby, her large aluminum dishpan. The innovative umbrella shielded Kimberly from the furious downfall washing over the dishpan and spraying out in a dense waterfall.

I hurried to the end of the porch, meeting them as they stepped in out of the merciless onslaught. Mom handed Jack the unique umbrella, uncovering my peacefully sleeping baby. I broke down in thankful tears, taking my little daughter in my arms. She was perfectly dry except for one drop of water that fell from the dishpan onto her tiny little nose.

Our neighbors suffered many losses that horrible night. Some persons in surrounding communities even lost their lives. Yet thanks to God and my resourceful mother, the dishpan I hated in my youth had now earned a place of honor in my heart.

Printed in: *Seek,* April 17, 1994
Reprinted in The Sunday Gazette-Mail, June 2, 1996
Reprinted on Moonflower Ministry Web Site, May, 2002
Reprinted on The Sermon Illustrator, May, 2002

Thirty-eight years after the flood, Mom and Dad are the center of attention during a family reunion at Kim's house

Irreplaceable

God dipped a brush in golden sunlight,
Giving a mother's face a smile,
Encouragement for children fainting
From the burden of stressful trials.
Two brilliant stars God borrowed from
Sweep of azure evening skies,
Alight with the glory of His heaven;
These would become a mother's eyes.
Glad song of bird and gurgling brook
Slipped into a mother's throat,
Assured sweetest lullabies,
Love whispered in each note.
God gave a mother two good ears,
Always attuned to the slightest cry
Of children who, in dark of night,
On her nearness could rely.
God made a mother's arms, though strong,
Soft and gentle at the same time,
A sickbed for an ailing child,
Cradled safe, secure, sublime.
From ministering angels, always serving,
God patterned two tireless feet,
For mothers who, without complaint,
Serve their family's every need.
Last, from depths of His own heart
God scooped out handfuls of love,
Kneaded soft as a summer cloud,
Warm as the feathered breast of a dove.
Then clothing His creation in patience,
Endowing her with forgiving grace,
God convinced us no one on earth
Can ever take a mother's place.

Before Mom's death, we talked a lot on the phone. She did more of the talking; I did more of the listening. A busy woman, sometimes I became extremely frustrated at the length of the mostly one-sided conversations, but how glad I am now that I took the time to listen. God took the time to listen to Mom, too, as the following story reveals.

Valentines with Roots

...with lavish kindness the gifts of God are strown,
Bishop Reginald Heber 1783-1826

My elderly mother busied herself one fine fall day, cracking walnuts, picking out sweet, juicy nutmeats and storing them in the freezer for winter use. "I sure got my exercise walking down the field and back every day," she told me with a chuckle one afternoon on the phone. "I wore myself out checking the ground for those fallen walnuts."

She told me she considered the trees a blessing, other than a way to remain active. "I mentioned to your father one day that I wished I had walnuts like we had in the past," she said. "We called them butternuts. The nutmeats were larger, whiter, and sweeter than regular walnuts. Not long after that," she continued, "your father came from a walk down by the riverbank, grinning like a possum. 'Louise,' he asked, 'what do you think I found down there on the far side of the field?'

"He took me down and showed me. Young walnut trees. Three of them. Sure enough, the nutmeats were white and delicious and easy to shell. I think God heard me ahead of time," my mother mused. "He had those trees growing for me to discover after I voiced my wish."

"Could be," I replied. "Doesn't it say somewhere in the Bible that God gives us the desires of our hearts? If we delight in doing His will," I added.

Mom told me how my youngest sister, Debbie, had voiced her desire for a wisteria, then found one growing in her back yard. That reminded me of a floral wish of my own. "Remember how many redbuds bordered our yard when we first moved here?" I asked. "They were so beautiful, backed by the green pines and white dogwoods. But for some reason, they all died out. We found a young one farther up the road and planted it in the yard, but it died, too.

"One day I said to Jack, 'I'd sure like to be able to get a redbud to grow.' Then one morning the next spring, while washing dishes, I noticed a strange, tall plant in the wildflower bed outside my window. I hurried to see what it was and found my wish granted."

I explained to my mother how my heart's desire grew vigorously that first year, bearing heavy foliage of familiar, heart-shaped leaves. "Looking at them," I said, "I pictured the heart of God. Each one seemed to me as if it were a valentine sent straight from Heaven, proclaiming His love."

"Well, just maybe He'll give you a walnut tree some day, too," Mom said with a chuckle.

"That would *have* to come from God," I told her. "Remember the big one that grew by the side of the yard when we first moved here? It died, and Jack had to cut it down. Later, we planted fourteen seedlings out on the pipeline ridge, but they all died, too. I didn't get my wish on a walnut tree," I told my mother before I hung up, "but I'm glad you got yours."

The next spring, Jack and I planted flowers around our patio, spicy orange marigolds and dainty purple and white alyssum backed by faithful perennials, multi-colored irises, variegated hostas, lavender statice, and pink bleeding heart. One day I reached for a weed, previously hidden from sight until it sprouted into view above the marigolds. *Hmmm! Those leaves look familiar,* I told myself.

Digging my fingers into the soft, black loam, I carefully dug soil away from one side of the green, tender stalk until I discovered what I was sure would lie at the base of the plant. I uncovered an aromatic walnut, buried deep and safe in its bed, the dark, corrugated seed swollen and cracked by moisture. The fertilizer I applied to my flowers had evidently speeded the walnut seedling's growth.

How did the walnut get there? We had no walnut trees on our twelve acres, and we hadn't brought in any nuts for years. Jack carefully dug up my buried treasure and planted it in an open space where it could grow unimpeded.

My walnut tree displayed no heart-shaped leaves. It whispered no words of endearment. But the black, decaying seed had taken root, sending up a message of love through the rich earth. I passed it each day to empty scraps on our compost pile, and it spoke loudly and clearly to me, a reminder of the promise I had mentioned to my mother of God giving us our heart's desire.

Today, we have two walnut trees. My husband and I found another that year, growing in the same flowerbed. Last year, Jack cracked out the first walnuts, the main ingredient in a nut topping for Thanksgiving pumpkin pie. I thought of how appropriate it was to eat our first dessert from our wished-for gift on Thanksgiving, a day set aside in gratitude for God's blessings.

Does God really listen with a caring ear to secret yearnings, loving us so much He delights in fulfilling such unusual desires? I believe He does. Don't we delight in giving our children not only their needs, but also their wants? One thing I do know, I always look forward to spring, when the lovely, lavender-laden branches of the redbud outside my kitchen window remind me that, when we turn our hearts toward God, He rewards us in many wonderful ways.

Quotation from:
THE OXFORD DICTIONARY OF QUOTATIONS
Third Edition
Oxford University Press copyright 1979

Printed in *The Sunday Gazette-Mail,* February 28, 1999

I inherited my love of nature from Mom and Dad. In this photo, Jack and Dad walk the Beartown trail, a place where nature abounds.

DAD TAKES CHARGE

The time came when Mom could no longer take charge of a situation as she did in the flood. Now it was Dad's turn.

In the Eye of the Storm

The call came late in the night. My husband was working night shift. I was deep in sleep when the phone rang. Recognizing my brother's voice, I knew something was wrong. "Mom's had a stroke," he said. "She's in the hospital. Dad and Becky are with her. No need for you to go. I think everything's under control, but I just wanted you to know."

Not go? How could I not go? This was my mother. Suddenly, although she was in her seventies and I in my fifties, I was a child again, needing the assurance of her presence. I called my husband, dressed, and drove the thirty miles through the dark and lonely night to the hospital.

I found my father and sister-in-law in the emergency waiting room. They directed me to a room where a team of medical personnel worked to stabilize Mom before moving her to a private room. A nurse filled me in on her condition. My mother was bleeding in the center of the brain, a place inaccessible to surgery. We could only pray the bleeding would stop.

Allowed only a few moments with Mom, I hurried back to the waiting room. My father seemed perfectly calm, but he looked so vulnerable, so alone. Yet I felt the strength of his presence. He told me Mom had fallen to the floor, disoriented and unable to get up. He struggled to help her, but every movement only intensified her nausea and dizziness. He called my brother, who phoned for an ambulance. "They worked for three-and-a-half hours to stabilize her enough to get her into the ambulance," Dad told me.

17

A doctor came through the emergency room doors. A young, compassionate man, he knelt before my father. "Mr. Miller," he said, "I can't give you any hope right now. Your wife's not doing well. It could go either way."

"Of course, you can't give me hope," my father replied, placing his gnarled hand on the soft, white one that rested on his knee. "Don't misunderstand me," he continued in a gentle voice. "I realize you are very learned and dedicated to your profession, and I mean no offense, but it's not up to you. It's all up to my Father in Heaven. My hope lies in Him, and I say my wife will be fine. I asked God to take care of her, and I know He will."

The physician, taken aback and at a loss for words, patted my father's hand, excused himself, and left. Seven hours later, we were told that Mom would be moved. The bleeding had stopped. We could follow her to her room and quietly visit. Morning had come. Two of my sisters had joined us in the waiting room. A third called intermittently from her place of employment. We all followed the bed into the elevator, relieved and in high spirits.

Our hopes plummeted when Mom was suddenly rushed from the elevator to the NICU. The move had started the bleeding again. We were sent to the NICU waiting room where we spent another several hours expecting Mom to die. She was seventy-one. Was I ready to let her go?

No. I was frantic with concern. But, in the midst of our worry, my seventy-six-year-old father sat composed and trusting. His calmness touched us all.

My mother survived. She suffered no speech defect, no paralysis, but recovery was slow. Disoriented and weak, she came home, after seven weeks therapy, supplied with a cane, a bathtub chair, and plans for a daily nurse. She ignored the cane, the chair, and our pleas for the nurse. She rebelled at any overtures on our part to care for her house. She entrusted herself completely to the care of my father, just as he had entrusted her to the care of his Father.

Today Mom is nearly her old self again, but my parents' roles have reversed since the beginning of her illness. Dad takes full care of the house, cooking and cleaning and attentively watching over my mother while she putters about, occupying herself with menial tasks. The day may come when my father will no longer be here or be able to care for his wife. Then it may be my turn.

But, if and when the time comes, I pray I will remember the lesson I've learned from him. In the midst of our trials, we must call on God to do His part. Then we do ours, calmly, patiently, lovingly, and without complaint, but most of all, with trust in the One who has it all under control.

Just as Jesus calmed the raging storm on the Sea of Galilee when the disciples called on Him, He stands ready to answer our cry for help. He may not always speak, "Peace, be still!" to the tempest that tosses us about, but He will allow us to dwell in the eye of the storm. There His peace abides — a peace that can only be spoken into existence by our loving Savior and attained by our trust in Him.

Printed in *The Sunday Gazette-Mail,* February 4, 1996

MOM'S TURN AGAIN

The day came when Dad could no longer care for Mom. We were losing the father we knew to dementia.

Home, Sweet Home

And we won't go home till morning.
J. B. Buckstone 1802-1879

I knew there was a problem the day my parents came on a customary visit. Dad sat on the couch, sunlight through the window at his back glinting off his silvery hair. Deep in thought, his delft-blue eyes puzzled, he asked, "Jack, if you were me, which direction would you go to get home?"

The next visit, my father stopped at a convenience store to ask directions. "Why, Frank, don't you know how to get to Nancy's house?" my concerned mother asked.

"I just want to make sure," Dad replied. This, after thirty-five years of driving the route between our home and theirs. Mom's concern grew when she followed Dad inside the store and overheard him asking directions to our place, giving another man's name.

We drove my parents home that night, Jack and Dad in their old maroon Buick, Mom and I following in our vehicle. "Dad's confused a lot lately," Mom revealed to me. "He passed up our driveway the other day, insisting the house wasn't ours. I finally convinced him it was."

Dad's condition worsened. One night, he wanted to gather up all their belongings and get out of "that old couple's way and go home." Hospitalized for a stroke, he didn't recognize the visiting grandchildren and his son. He told the doctors Mom was eighteen with three small children and kept insisting a car parked on the therapy verandah, visible from the lobby, was his. Frenzied, he tried to figure a way to get through the glass wall down to the car so he could go home.

Dad kept wanting to go home. The hospital staff found him one day, his street clothes bundled in his arms, wandering an upper floor, trying to escape. Dad has been trying to get home since, never realizing where home might be, never satisfied when he is there.

The next time my parents came to visit, we went to pick them up, our trunk packed with suitcases and medicines, something alien to Dad. He had lived eighty-four years in the best of health. Between his last visit and this one, he had suffered two strokes and a heart attack. Doctors had diagnosed Parkinson's Disease and possible Alzheimer's.

Mom had always been content with long visits, Dad restless when the sun set. Now they were both reluctant to stay. After months of tears and frustration, alternately living with three of their five children, we agreed with the doctor that it was far better for them to be happy than healthy.

Mom struggles with Dad's confusion, but is glad to be home. Dad is still not content. Every evening, when bedtime nears, he dons a red-and-green toboggan and faded work jacket and tells Mom, "Time to go!" She usually talks him out of it, but three times he escaped Mom's vigilance, searching for a place he will never find on this earth.

"I've cried buckets of tears," my mother tells me, breaking my heart. Each time Dad escapes, Mom's prayers bring him back, twice on his own, once escorted by two angels, one extremely tall, the other as extremely short, in an old blue car. At least we considered them angels.

That night was cold, and Dad had fallen by the roadside, badly skinning his hands and head. Automobile lights glowing off his silver hair saved him. Luckily lucid in a necessary moment, he told the men his address.

Before Dad's failing health, gardening was his passion. He plowed and planted from early spring till late fall, growing hothouse plants in between. He could expound on the properties of growing tomatoes for hours at a time, a subject that used to bore me nearly to tears. Now I just wish I could hear him do it again.

No one ever left Mom and Dad's house in the growing months without a tour of the garden and yard and an armload of bounty. My favorite was the leafy green lettuce and tender green onions. My husband says I make the best wilted lettuce of anyone he knows. I owe that particular talent to Dad's generosity. He has supplied excellent, organic ingredients for many years.

Gardening is still Dad's passion, but only a panacea for his occasional restlessness. The last garden he and my brother planted together, he haphazardly harvested before growth had hardly begun, pulling onions as mere seedlings and digging potatoes the size of marbles. "Let him go," Mom said. "It keeps him content." This year, my brother used the land to plant a garden of his own.

In the early spring, I went for a visit, a hard thing to do anymore, wondering which visit might be the time that my father wouldn't know me. I sat on the front porch with Dad for a while, he in a white wicker swing and me in a cushioned lawn chair. He told me about all the houses he owned and about how he needed to go see about them and about his home miles away, all illusions. Dad's vacant stare, his silent escapes into recesses of his mind where we can't follow, are no less heartbreaking than his confused ramblings.

Before our visit ended, Mom took us on the traditional yard and garden tour. Dad followed, shoulders slumped, shuffling slowly along behind us. He stood staring vacantly out over the field, seemingly far away, while Mom pointed out each flower in bloom.

Suddenly Dad seemed to awaken. He straightened, looked at me with recognition, and took me by the arm. "Come over here, Nancy," he said, leading me to my brother's garden with his old familiar jaunty step. Tall, proud onions marched along in single file between rows of gigantic leaves of perky spring green lettuce, a healthy contrast to Dad's feeble and confused efforts the year before.

"Let's pick you some lettuce and onions to take home," Dad said. "Weezy," he called to Mom (his endearment for Louise), "bring one of those plastic grocery bags to put some lettuce and onions in."

"But this is Bub's garden," I protested. "I don't want to pick anything without his permission." But Dad was determined. We picked companionably in the warm sun, his white hair shining, while he explained all the work he had done to grow such nice vegetables. He wasn't taking undue credit. In his mind that now lived in an earlier time, he had planted the garden, and without his excellent example and tutelage, his son's lettuce and onions could never have succeeded so well.

I later called my brother to apologize for pillaging his vegetable patch, but I really couldn't feel too sorry. For a few happy moments on a sunny spring afternoon, at his favorite occupation, I had my Dad back for a little while, and for the first time since his illness, he realized he was home. Wilted lettuce had never tasted so good.

COUNTDOWN

They sit at home,
Not visiting any more.
He forgets how to get there,
She forgets when it's time to leave.
Living in a litter of memories--
Old newspaper clippings,
Faded photographs and chipped mementos--
They refuse to part with one,
Their lives diminished enough.
She rarely cooks anymore.
He burns everything.
The television has faded into snow,
Their eyesight doing the same.
Nearly deaf, he sits in silence,
The radio a relic of the past,
As he feels he has become.
Handmade birdhouses and feeders,
Affixed to every tree-limb,
Have full occupancy.
Near death, they observe the living.
Each creature, adopted in place of children
Having flown the nest, is given a name.
Even squirrels that rob the feeders are welcome.
Chipmunks destroy the strawberries,
Deer and groundhog pillage the corn.
No matter. It doesn't take much for two.
With little else to do,
The habits of planting and gardening die hard.
They cling to vestiges of time,
Sensing the need to cherish and sustain
What remains of life,
A rare commodity,
Nearly spent.

My brother called one day just before Dad's release from the hospital after his stroke. Could I take Mom and Dad in? My testing had come. Would I remember the lesson Dad taught about patient caring with no complaints?

New Grace

We had a dear friend who used to sing the beautiful and encouraging song, "New Grace." This precious friend died unexpectedly at the age of fifty from a massive heart attack. I wasn't there to discover if our friend found that new grace in the long hours of his pain and suffering, but I believe he did. I know his wife did. I saw the evidence of God's new grace in her life as she often struggled with loneliness and depression, yet testified to God's comfort and nearness.

I discovered that new grace in a tremendous way myself when, a few years ago, my doctor told me she was sure I had incurable bone cancer. Peace and joy still wash over me when I think of the instant surcease of my symptoms and those days between the prognosis and the glad diagnosis, when God cradled my head on His bosom and Heaven became a thrilling expectancy. God did indeed give new grace.

I experienced that new grace again just recently, when I took my aging parents into my home for a month to care for them. A private person, who thrives on being alone and delving into my writing and other creative arts, I was flooded with insecurity and doubt when my brother called, asking if I could care for Mom and Dad for a while. My spirit was more than willing, but my physical and emotional self trembled at the thought.

I've never been a good nurse, as my children can testify, nor a good housekeeper, and my physical endurance is weak. I also have never been a good host. Although I love people, constant companionship wearies me. Without private time, my blood pressure shoots up and my nerves fray, a common occurrence with creative people. This used to make me feel selfish, but I now realize God made us all for a certain purpose. If I were not the way I am, I could not spend days by myself writing and composing songs for His glory. Now I asked myself, "How will I cope, with curtailed freedom and my presence in constant demand?"

Mulling the situation over a few days later, I prayed, "God, I can't do this in myself. I love my parents, and I want to help, but I can't change my personality. Please give me grace to face this challenge."

"If ye shall ask anything in my name, I will do it," Jesus promised in John 14:14 KJV. *"If ye love me, keep my commandments,"* was the condition he added in verse fifteen. One of God's commandments is to honor our mother and father. I had no other choice but to trust and obey. I asked in Jesus' name, and He did it.

Oh, I got weary, and at times I yearned for privacy and time to do my own thing. It's good to be alone again, but I will always cherish the weeks I had with my mother and father. I will never forget precious moments when our hearts flowed as one, or the times I saw into my parents' souls as I had never seen before.

There was the morning I found my mother sobbing on the couch, and I sat down and sobbed with her, my arms around her. She knew her life was forever changed, and my heart ached for her. If I could have changed things, I would have, but like Dad had told the doctor years before, it wasn't up to me.

Mom and I washed dishes together, companionably picked berries and peaches, and worked together to renew one of her old hobbies, crocheting. We may have ripped more stitches than we ended with, but, as with life, the finished product is what is important.

There were the peaceful, ambling walks and quiet conversations I had with my father. As I slowed my pace to match his, slipped shoes on his feet and buttoned his shirts, I thought of all the times he slowed his steps to match mine and worked at two jobs to allow me shoes and clothing. As I watched him clear my woods path of fallen limbs, I thought of all the times he had worked to clear my life's path of obstacles that threatened to hinder me.

New grace. It's really not a new grace, but God's continual and eternal grace held in reserve and given just when we need it. My parents are back home now, with my oldest sister caring for them. We all know things will never be as they were, and all our days are numbered. But when the time comes for more catastrophic changes, I know God will generously pour out grace in abundant supply.

Like the bad-tasting cod liver oil my mother used to spoon into our mouths, we may sometimes rebel and shudder at what life deals us, but the benefits are always there beneath the bad taste.

Are you facing an ordeal you feel is too big a challenge, or going through one that you feel will break you? Hold to God's promise of grace in the time of need. He'll cry with you and cradle you in His arms. He'll walk with you and clear your path of obstructions. He'll knit back what Satan rips out. He'll slip stout spiritual shoes on your feet and clothe you in grace. He'll give you an expectancy of Heaven to override your dread of death.

I said in the beginning of this column that "I had a dear friend . . ." I want to change that to, "I *have* a dear friend." We never lose a friend who trusts Jesus to take Him to Heaven. God cares for our departed friends and loved ones much more tenderly and patiently than I could ever care for my parents. The time will come when, with new grace, He will allow us all to meet again. See you there?

Printed in *The Sunday Gazette-Mail,* August 16, 1998

Mom and Dad stand behind us, as they always did. Jack and I are almost hidden by eight of our ten grandchildren.

Mom and Me, Peeling an Onion

Life's sharp knife peels
our mother/daughter relationship
like an onion.
Holding my first child in my arms,
the knife of instant perception strips away
the impenetrable outer layer
of my resentment and anger,
thin inner layers of misunderstandings.
My mother's helplessness,
her reaching out,
after her stroke,
is a knife of fear,
gouging out my deep hard core of bitterness,
recognized almost too late as waste,
now discarded forever.
The sharp blade of Dad's Alzheimer's
slices too deeply, suddenly,
piercing both Mom's heart and mine
until they bleed.
Stripped layer by layer,
my mother and I shed tears
as the knife of fate cuts on,
wasting, diminishing,
The knife of joint pain serrates
through layers of my former ignorance
of her maternal sacrifices,
my carelessness of her emotions,
childish ungratefulness
and callous disregard.
The sharpened knife strips on, layer by layer,
until all that remains
is a small, tight inner circle
of togetherness
and a pungent aroma of love that clings,
and will linger
beyond death.

A Walk with Dad

The sun, sifting like fine golden wheat
Through limb and leaf,
Spatters the moss-green forest floor.
Turning, I wait,
Mesmerized by the shimmer of sunlight,
Scintillating on locks of silver-white hair.
Slowly shuffling, shoulders slumped,
Dad smiles,
Eyes as bright as delft porcelain.
Face twisted, limbs weakened
By paralytic stroke,
With effort, he stoops,
Lifting with arthritic hands
Fallen limbs obstructing our path.
Our progress slows,
His mind caught in repetition,
Intent on yanking free each tangled branch,
Gnarled hands tossing aside each tiny twig
Marring our daily walk.
Patiently, I wait,
Giving in to his sudden industry.
Does he recapture,
In this labor or love,
A feeling of purpose?
I only know he has recaptured for me
Faded memories of childhood
When, just as intently,
He worked at freeing
Obstructions hindering my walk in
The pathway of life.

MOM TAKES CHARGE AGAIN

When my sister, Eleanor, had to go home for a while, Mom and Dad stayed with me. Mom finally rebelled. "We want to stay home," she stubbornly insisted. So I went there to care for them until my sister's return.

Dad's Bouquet

When my children were small, they loved to bring me bouquets, as most children do. The three girls picked dandelions, daisies, or any other flower that happened to be in bloom at the time. Jim, my only son, looked at Mother Nature with a different eye. He brought me treasures only a small boy in love with nature could produce: pocketfuls of squashed earthworms, a collection of tiny acorns, handfuls of rustling, brown leaves.

Mothers aren't choosy, unless it comes to Jiff®. Beauty is in the eye of the beholder, and if Jim's eye considered his offerings suitable, to me they were as beautiful as the girls more colorful offerings. I always arranged Jim's leaves in a vase, displaying them on the dinner table, or kept the acorns in a bowl until emerging larva forced trashing them. Of course, the worms were a different story.

My children all too soon grew up and moved away from home. Their offerings became more sophisticated: an exquisite handmade or purchased gift, an occasional single rose, or a professionally arranged floral bouquet from a shop. On one end of the spectrum, the children had attained adulthood. On the other end, my aging father was becoming more childish, the result of dreaded Alzheimer's Disease.

Roles reversed. My children managed families and jobs and didn't need constant mothering anymore. Dad lost control of his faculties and claimed, for a time, the attention I once gave my children. Staying at my house, he had to be helped into his clothing. He often had to be shown where to retire for the night and how to get under the covers.

I once caught Dad shaving with a bar of guest soap. Another time, he appeared at the breakfast table, squeezed into my slacks and wearing one of my blouses — backwards. He brushed his teeth from time to time with his hairbrush and combed his hair with the bath brush.

Dad always arose at five in the morning, bathing in the nude at the bathroom sink until I found him chilled to the bone and led him back to bed. This early morning ritual often depleted our well. Many times we resorted to bottled water and carrying clothes back to my parents' home to launder, but the irritation never depleted the deep love and compassion eternally welling up in my heart for my father.

Dad was never hungry when you asked, but stood before the opened refrigerator door searching for food if you delayed meal preparation an instant. Anything you placed on his plate disappeared and brought extravagant praise, no matter how simply prepared. Dad had lost his reasoning, but not his good manners

If Dad tired in walking, he just fell to the ground where he stood. It took all my strength to get him on his feet again when he was rested, but I always thought of the many times in my married life when he had helped my husband and me get back on our feet. I didn't mind the strain. I just stood by him until he was ready to go on again. After all, he had always stood by me, as a child, in my weak moments and suffered the strain of my young adult years.

Mom and Dad finally got settled back in their home after his two strokes and a heart attack, with my older sister caring for them. When duties called the sister temporarily away, Mom and Dad resided at my house. Once, I went to theirs for nine days, preparing meals, doing housework, and watching over Dad, who loved to putter in his garden or walk the bottomland by the river.

Dad came in one afternoon with an unusual bouquet for me, taking me back in time to the days when my little boy did the same. Handing me the handful of dried, brown catalpa leaves, he said, with the enthusiasm and delight that little Jim always presented his gifts, "I picked these for you. I thought you might like them. Aren't they pretty and shiny?"

He was right on both counts. They were pretty and shiny, and I did like them. The leaves, placed in an old dented, silver-plated urn, gave a bright touch to the dinner table, as far as I was concerned. Of course, beauty *is* in the eye of the beholder. Later, Mom asked if I wanted her to throw the leaves out.

"No, not yet," I said. "Leave them. I think they look nice." She looked at me askance, perhaps wondering if I had inherited Dad's illness, but she left the leaves. I think she knew that it was more the warm feeling they gave me than the eye appeal that made me want to preserve my gift.

When I went back to visit after my sister's return, I noticed my bouquet had disappeared. I suppose Eleanor had tossed them. I couldn't blame her. In her eyes, not being the recipient, they had no worth. Some things, like squashed earthworms and old dead catalpa leaves, have to be personally received from the hands of an innocent heart to realize their value. I wish I had brought my bouquet home.

MOM CAN'T KEEP UP

I came home from church October 8ᵗʰ, 2000 to find Jack, who had gone to another church with a friend, anxiously pacing the floor. "Your Dad is missing," he said. "Hurry and change into warm clothes so we can go help look for him."

A Journey I Didn't Want to Take

Sometimes life takes us down paths we don't want to travel. My eighty-six-year-old father wandered away from home Sunday evening. It is now Friday morning as I write this column, and he hasn't been found. The nights have been so cold and my heart so heavy thinking about him alone, confused, and hungry. I don't want to think he might be dead.

My three-year-old grandson Stone told his mother, "Don't worry, Mommy. Jesus will come and put a warm blanket over Pappaw and take care of him." Then he added, "Do you think he'll know Pappaw Gene when he gets there?" Stone was referring to his paternal grandfather who passed away earlier. Stone came to my mother's house last night and told her, "I'm praying to Jesus for Pappaw."

So many are praying. I don't know how we could bear this uncertainty without the outpouring of love from friends, family, and strangers. If my father were here to see it, he would praise the Lord for love and grace, shown through mankind. I do the same.

My parents came to stay with me for a while when my father was recuperating from pneumonia, two strokes, and a heart attack in June of 1998. He and I took a walk one day out my woods path while Mom rested. The sun, sifting like strands of fine golden wheat through tree branches sheltering my path, spattered the green moss floor and shimmered from his full head of white hair. Slowly shuffling, shoulders slumped, Dad looked up at me with bright blue eyes when I removed a fallen limb from his path. He smiled, his face twisted a little from temporary paralysis. He stooped, tossing every little twig and branch that obstructed our path into the woods on either side. I patiently waited, our progress slowed considerably. My father has always been a hardworking man, and I knew he found purpose in this labor of love.

His sudden industry took me back to childhood, when he encouraged my Christian walk and helped clear my life's path from hindrances. My father hasn't been a perfect man. He told me once that God showed him how reprobate he was, and he determined to learn from that lesson. He learned well. If you looked the world over, you wouldn't find a finer Christian, a more humble and thoughtful man.

Now it seems we are looking the world over for my father. Fliers have been distributed over the state, perhaps beyond. E-mails requesting prayer have been sent worldwide. TV and radio stations have alerted the public. Calls come from miles away, and the Sissonville Volunteer Fire Department has followed up every lead. Search and Rescue dogs, family, and volunteers have combed the hills, creeks, and riverbanks, and state and local police are involved. My mother's home has been filled to overflowing with food, friends, family, and love.

The days have been long and hard, but the evenings when the sun sets are the hardest to bear. I feel the chill creeping in, and I worry about my father. Due to his age and the Coumadin® he takes to thin his blood, he has always been so cold. I want my father home or with Jesus, not wandering out there alone, confused, and freezing. I look for him everywhere. Would you please do the same? And pray for my mother. She and my father have been together for sixty-four years. A part of her is missing.

Printed in *The Jackson Herald*, October 18, 2000

FALSE HOPE

So many false rumors. The following story is of a rumor I have never been able to reason out. Would someone lie for sensationalism when hearts are so broken?

Dad, Where Are You?

As I write this column, my father has been missing for thirteen days. I was resigned that he might never be found, but Monday night we received a call that changed my mind. According to the caller, my father came to a woman's house in Gauley Bridge, Thursday or Friday, cold and hungry, mumbling something about getting to Hawk's Nest for a family reunion. She went to get him food, but when she returned he was gone. We were told she called 911.

I had promised my parents we would take them to Hawk's Nest for a picnic in October. Mom misunderstood and thought I meant the following weekend. She and Dad got ready and waited. When no one showed up, Mom told Dad we had forgotten, that they wouldn't be going after all.

The next day, Dad left home. It all fit so well. The reaction of the Search and Rescue dogs gave the authorities the assumption that Dad had been given a ride soon after he left home. We had earlier calls about sightings in Marmet and Malden, towns along the route to Hawk's Nest. These reports proved most likely false, but how could we be sure?

Jack and I hardly slept that night. I'm sure none of my family did. The next day, we exhausted every avenue trying to locate the woman. Jack and I drove to Gauley Bridge and were horrified to discover the state police there had only been notified of the incident that morning. There had been no search. Had it been a hoax? How could it be?

Jack and I searched Gauley Bridge and Hawk's Nest. We traveled the entire route to Ansted, then back through Clay and down Interstate 79, posting more fliers. Most people had heard of Dad missing. We found everyone to be kind and concerned, but discovered nothing. This morning was the hardest morning I have faced since Dad's disappearance; to be given hope, then have it snatched away is so disheartening.

Thanksgiving is approaching. Mom and Dad often come to my house for the celebration. I recall thinking last year how grateful I was that they were here, our house running over with twenty-five happy people. If Dad could only be with us again this year, what a thanksgiving that would be!

But if not, we still have much to be thankful for. Mom and Dad spent many holidays and vacations with us, walking with us on nature trails. I noticed them slowing each year. Our last trip together, their hips hurt and they were exhausted for days. That's why I planned the family reunion at Hawk's Nest, a short distance, yet nature abounded there. Mom and Dad love nature.

Although our family reunion at Hawk's Nest with Dad may never become reality, there will soon be a family reunion. Our steps are slowing, too, our life's journey nearly done. If Dad is gone, he has merely outdistanced us.

Hawk's Nest is a beautiful place, but Paul the Apostle wrote in I Corinthians 2:9 KJV, "*Eye hath not seen, nor ear heard, neither have entered into the heart of man, the things which God hath prepared for them that love him.*" Dad loved God above everything. He taught his children to do the same. God is preparing a place for us.

Driving to Hawk's Nest, I fantasized about driving up and seeing Dad sitting patiently on a picnic table. "Where have you been?" he'd ask with that big smile and his blue eyes bright. "I've been waiting." Maybe he's waiting for us now in Heaven. If so, I know he's smiling.

Printed in *The Jackson Herald, October 25, 2000*

Dad thoroughly enjoyed humor. At his seventieth birthday party at my house, he's ready to chow down on the "hot dog" my sister Sheila made for him.

HOPE SPRINGS ETERNAL

We could not forget Hawk's Nest. Could Dad have headed in that direction? Could he be there, wandering the road or mountainous hills, looking for us? We decided to go.

In Every Valley, I Find a Higher Plain

A few members of my family made an impromptu visit Saturday to Hawk's Nest. Before Dad's disappearance, we had planned a family reunion there. I felt Mom needed a change and asked her on Friday if she'd like to go. She said yes. Someone mentioned how bad the traffic would be because it was Bridge Day. We decided against it.

At nine-thirty that night, my younger sister called. She would be going to the Bridge celebration to pass out fliers about Dad. "Hawk's Nest is only nine or ten miles away," she said. I thawed a turkey in the microwave, plopped it in the crockpot, made some dressing, and baked a peach pie. My older sister made potato and fruit salad, and the younger cooked green beans. We left at ten the next morning.

We met many nice people who took fliers and promised to pray for Dad. I think we all secretly hoped for some miracle, but in spite of disappointment, we enjoyed our time together. I remarked how odd it is that it took a family separation to bring a family together. My Mom, brother, three sisters, and I have spent more time together lately than we have in years. We've received encouraging calls and visits from friends and relatives we rarely hear from, some calls from strangers who have become friends.

Jack and I attended church Saturday after arriving home. The Joy Beams sang a song that stated, "In every valley there is a higher plain." I have experienced that this month. Although we are walking through a low, dark valley, God's Holy Word, the love, support, and concern of family, friends, and strangers have lifted us from our valley of heartache and wondering to a higher plain of hope and endurance.

It wasn't coincidence that I read Psalm 139 the morning before Dad disappeared. The scripture touched me so much. I read it to the church congregation that Sunday night just minutes after Dad ran away. Coming home to find him gone, I found great comfort in recalling this Psalm, which speaks of God's loving presence, no matter where you are.

Verse eleven really moved me. *"If I say, surely the darkness shall cover me; even the night shall be light about me."* I thought of those long, cold nights, and knew Dad's faith in God would lighten his darkness. About a week before Dad disappeared, I came upon Psalms 71 and claimed it for him and myself. This chapter speaks of God not forsaking us in our old age. This scripture also came to mind that first night when sleep was the farthest thing from my mind.

"Why so many prayers and no answer?" some have asked. I have to be truthful and say I've asked it, too. Only God knows the answer. I do know my father would be willing to suffer if his suffering brought about more love, drew his family closer together, directed someone to Christ, or made a difference in someone's life. His disappearance has done all that. And I know he hasn't suffered alone. God has surely been with him, just as He's been with us.

Satan may think he's triumphing, but we were assured victory many years ago when Dad chose to live his life for God. Dad is spiritually safe. We hope with all our hearts that he is also physically safe. The Joy Beams sang another song, "How long till this battle is over?" This is another question we ask. Please pray that our answer will come soon.

Printed in *The Jackson Herald*, November 1, 2000

SHARING OUR SORROW

Thanksgiving approached. Would we have Dad with us? If not, we would still have much for which to be thankful.

A Special Thanks to Those Who Have Cared and Shared

Several years ago, my daughter-in-law shared an Amish Friendship Bread starter and recipe with me. The starter had to be divided every ten days, each division supplying two loaves of variety bread. The remaining three-fourths were to be divided among friends. I appreciated the gift but wondered if Jack and I would (or should) devour all those calories, or if I could find three friends willing to share my starter.

The tenth day happened to fall on the day our church ladies began a monthly Bible Study. I baked two loaves of walnut-raisin bread, wrapping one of the warm, cinnamon-spiced creations to share with my spiritual sisters at the church's recreational building.

We broke this bread together while breaking the Bread of Life. My daughter Kim, who furnished the coffee and tea for our study, took a starter home with her. Daughter-in-law Kim (yes, two Kims) also took a starter. With four children, you can't have too many loaves of Friendship Bread.

This happened on a Thursday. On Saturday, Mom and Dad, seventy-five and eighty-one at the time, and still going strong, dropped in for a visit. I shared a slice of the bread with them. Dad liked it so well, Mom took a starter home. Now I was back where I started — with one starter.

When I realized the next dividing and baking day for my starter would fall during a scheduled writer's conference, I called daughter-in-law Kim, who lived next door at the time. Yes, she would baby-sit my starter. I added the sugar, milk, and flour and dropped it off before I left, supplying her with

41

the remaining ingredients for baking. She shared the three loaves and a new starter with me on my return.

Sharing. Isn't that what life is all about? Our family has not only shared Amish Friendship Bread and starter, but we've shared good times, laughter and joy, bad times, tears and sorrow over the years. Just like the Friendship bread, love is multiplied among us when we add the right ingredients to the relationships and are patient for the results. And we can never have too much. No matter how much love we give away, it will grow until there is plenty enough to go around, warm and sweet, filled with good fruits and spicing up our lives.

In the past six weeks, people have shared their love, time, thoughts, and gifts with me, heaped up, shook down, and running over. I had someone tell me once that God only gives back in the measure we give. I have to disagree, and I have proof that I am right. I have always been a rather selfish person, especially with my time and energy.

God doesn't take this into consideration, especially when He poured out His blessings on me these last two months. If I had received as I had given, the offerings may have been scant, but I have found abundant offerings of love and concern, so abundant that I feel guilty about the meager offerings I have given.

Tomorrow is Thanksgiving. It's good to have this avenue to thank so many of you and to express gratitude to God for all His blessings. A pastor from Gauley Bridge called today to say he was praying that Dad, God willing, would be with us Thanksgiving Day. God will answer that prayer, if not with Dad's physical presence, with his spirit and fond memories among us. God bless you and yours this Thanksgiving.

Printed in *The Jackson Herald, November* 22, 2000

DAD LEFT, BUT HE LEFT A LEGACY

Dad taught us all to love God and trust Him. How could we bear these days without this legacy Dad left behind?

If You Love Roses, You'll Soon Bear the Prick of Thorns

Sweeping my patio a few days ago, I noticed our rose bushes were all bare except one. This bush, in spite of freezing temperatures, bore a single crimson bud, brilliant against the drab background of a garden put to bed for the winter. Shivering in shirtsleeves from the frigid temperature, I hurried to get a closer look. Cupping the perfectly formed, fragile bud, unmarred by blight or insect bite, in my hand, I experienced awe along with the prick of thorns. I felt blessed, as if God had caused that one perfect rose to bloom in winter merely to brighten my day.

Later, I checked my e-mail. A caring friend had forwarded a message about rose stems, barren of buds as the other rose bushes in my garden. But these stems weren't bare due to winter's approach. They had been denuded of roses for a purpose — a reminder to customers who purchased them at a florist shop that we must suffer thorns in life if it is to be filled with roses.

In a rose garden, roses mature, fade, and fall, disintegrating again into the soil from which they came. From this enrichment, new shoots grow, new buds form. In spite of storms, insects, and blight, the ritual continues. New beauty springs forth from the old.

In life, loved ones mature, fade, and return to the soil. The closer our association with these loved ones, the more we are blessed with their beauty. But getting close also means a more painful prick, a more profuse bleeding of our hearts when they're gone. But the unfolding of their days, the flowering of their years, leaves behind an enrichment that helps new buds form into a thing of beauty. The ritual continues. No one lives and dies without leaving behind a little of himself or herself in each person they meet.

I think God did allow that one perfect rose to bloom just for me. Somehow, it made me think of Dad. It took the life and death of the mature roses to cause the new bud to form. Dad left a little of himself behind in all that he met. I can see him in each of my siblings. I know he left something valuable in me. He taught me to trust God, to praise Him in spite of thorns, to take time to worship Him. I hope when I fade and fall, I will have left a little of God behind in all my children and grandchildren.

I watch my three-year-old grandson, Stone, as he relates to my husband. On his visits, the first thing he wants to do is walk through our woods path with Pappaw, killing all the bears so Grandma can walk unafraid. On one walk, with Stone on his shoulders, Jack was praying. "Who are you talking to, Pappaw?" Stone asked. "I was talking to Jesus," Jack replied.

"Pappaw, I love you with all my heart!" Stone exclaimed. That's one thing that made me love Dad with all my heart. He had a close relationship with Jesus. He shouldered a lot of my burdens, but knew the day would come when his shoulders would weaken. So he made sure I knew Someone who could shoulder those burdens, who would "kill all the bears" so I could walk unafraid through this life. Dad enriched my life's soil with each mature petal of his days that fell. As I write this, today is Thanksgiving. Dad is gone, maybe never to return. But he's here in the family gathered around my dinner table. A little of him lives on in each of us.

Printed in *The Jackson Herald*, November 29, 2000

My Father

God took the strength of rugged trees,
The gentleness of lambs,
Mixed them up and carved them out
Into the shape of man.
He took the courage of the lion,
The peacefulness of doves,
Fashioned a father's heart from these,
And filled it full of love.
He stirred the calmness of the seas
With ocean's mighty waves,
Creating a father who could stand,
In trials, serene and brave.
He took the fury of the storm,
The brilliance of blue skies
And made a man who became a hero
In his children's eyes.
He took the wisdom of the ages,
The fortitude of time,
And made a father who could explain
Things without reason or rhyme.
And when the Father up in heaven
Completed this creation for earth,
He sent him down to be my dad,
A man of untold worth.

THANKSGIVING WITHOUT DAD

Dad didn't come home for Thanksgiving. We missed him, but recalling precious memories lightened our day.

Does Having A Full House Mean I'm a Winner?

I don't play Poker, but I do know having a full house this Thanksgiving made me a winner. My mother chose to spend the day with us, making a grand total of twenty-two. Jack went to pick her up while I wrote last week's column and finished preparing dinner. She was our first visitor, so we had time for quiet conversation before the doors burst open and the walls began bulging.

It's so heartwarming to have everyone together again, except Dad, of course. It's good to know that we contribute to the prosperity of grocers and turkey farmers. Turkey is not our only Thanksgiving tradition. We reminisce over funny fallacies of family members, mostly mine. Adding a new tradition this year, we recalled precious memories of Dad.

Mom spent the night, with expectations of attending Christmas Opening Day at Karen's Greenhouse in Ohio. The only problem was (I told you I was fallible), I got the dates mixed up. We still enjoyed our visit and purchased some beautiful poinsettias.

We took Mom home that afternoon, picking up two grandchildren. We took the children shopping on Saturday, then on Sunday took them and Mom to the Christmas Tree Exhibition at the Cultural Center (I got the date right this time). We spent an interesting afternoon, studying exhibits and crafts and viewing trees decorated in the tradition of twenty nations.

Tired, but happy, we dropped off the kids, then Mom. After a pit stop at home, we attended church. It felt good to relax afterwards, reading in bed, although the house seemed abnormally quite.

I look back, shake my head, and laugh when I recall all those unnecessary tears I shed when my family doctor and heart specialist told me that my heart condition ruled out children and the stress of housework. If anything would strain my heart, it would be wrestling down a twenty-two pound turkey to poke full of stuffing. Or the excitement of receiving countless bear hugs and kisses from grandkids taller than I am, or the overexertion of laughing at ridiculous reminisces and returning all those hugs and kisses. I think of what fun it would be, if I hadn't outlived my doctors, to invite them this Christmas and show them how God had proved them wrong.

When back in 1957, my hardworking father heard of my life-threatening condition, he threw down his tools and headed for the woods, where he fell on his knees and petitioned God in my behalf. Mom put in a bid for equal time. Arch Williams, elderly, white-haired pastor at Sugar Creek Community Mission at the time I bore my first child, was a prayer warrior, as were many of the church members. How could doctors' diagnoses stand up against all that onslaught of prayer?

Psalm 56:8 tells us that God stores our tears in bottles. Revelation 5:8 tells us that our prayers are kept in vials. Down through life, I have pictured God popping the cork on those bottles and vials and pouring out a portion of those fervent prayers and tears to ward off further prognoses of terminal bone cancer, heart ailments, and other diseases.

Matthew 20:2 advises us to ". . . *lay up for yourselves treasures in heaven.*" After listening, this past Thanksgiving, to some of my grandchildren's escapades I know it will take many tears to anoint them, many prayers to protect them down through life. I'd better close and take time to lay up another bottle and vial in heaven. I want each of their lives to be as wonderfully blessed and richly rewarding as God, through his loving grace, has allowed mine to be.

Printed in *The Jackson Herald*, December 6, 2000

Editing this column for the book, I thought of how nonchalant about Dad's absence we must have appeared to readers. Not so. When sorrow strikes, life doesn't stand still. And when family members get together, there is bound to be laughter and fun. But beneath the joy, the sorrow persisted. Also, I believe we were buoyed by false hope. So many had told us that they knew Dad was alive and well, perhaps living in a shelter or with someone who didn't realize his identity. If only we knew.

AND NOW THE TEARS

Mom always told us that if you laughed at the dinner table, you would cry the next morning. We laughed much during our Thanksgiving feast. Now it was time for the tears.

For Those Wondering about Dad

I found one of Dad's shirts Tuesday night. My spirits immediately plummeted. I'm a great procrastinator when it comes to ironing or mending. The pile had outgrown the closet, so I decided I'd better tackle it. Near the bottom, I came upon the shirt.

I found the shirt at Mom's just after Dad disappeared. She had left it out so she would remember to give it to me to repair. The cuff was ripped nearly off the sleeve. I slipped it out to the car, not wanting Mom to find it and grieve — silly perhaps, since all his other belongings are still in the house.

Speechless, I held the shirt out to Jack. "Your dad's shirt," he said. Numb, I nodded and carried it back to the bedroom. Standing there in the dark, with tears in my eyes, I buried my face in the shirt and breathed in Dad's scent. It made me remember a friend of mine carrying her husband's jeans around the day he died. Another time, I heard of a woman who cried for hours after someone washed her dead daughter's pillow, destroying the little girl's scent. Now I had a better understanding of how these women felt. It was almost as if Dad were still inside the shirt.

Only a little over five feet tall, Dad was hard to fit. I dreaded it when he needed new clothes. I love to create, but find it a chore to mend or alter. I would have to carefully rip the cuffs off his shirts, then cut several inches from the sleeve before reattaching them. The pants were easier. I just whacked them off several inches and hemmed them on the machine, except dress pants, which required handstitching.

If Dad were here today, I would joyfully mend his clothes. I never think of him but what I see him wearing tan Dickie® workshirts and pants, his favorites. He was wearing them the day he disappeared, and he wore them in the dream I had of him later. When it snowed so hard the other night, I couldn't sleep. Every time I closed my eyes, I pictured Dad lying out there in those thin workclothes, the snow slowly piling up on him. Mom called the next day and told me she didn't go to bed at all, but stayed up all night, reading her Bible, walking the floor, singing, and praying about Dad.

A friend called tonight and asked us to pray for her daughter, who didn't come in from school. Recalling the horror of that first night, my heart ached for the family. I prayed and ironed and ironed and prayed. I decided to ask Jack if we could go to their house to be with them, remembering how comforting their presence was to me when Dad disappeared. Then the phone rang. The girl had been found. If I would give this mother any advice, I would tell her to hug her daughter every day and breathe in that wonderful scent God gave especially to her.

I put Dad's shirt back in my closet. So many people have asked if Dad has been found. I wish I could tell them yes, but I can't. Someone told Mom yesterday, "Wouldn't it be nice if they found him in Florida, sitting in a beach chair, soaking up the sun and having the time of his life?"

I realize this woman wasn't serious, but I think she came close. I don't believe my father is in Florida, but I do believe he's alive and well, soaking up heaven's Son and having the time of his life. Dad's age and mental condition kept him from having a good time here. In spite of missing him so much, the best we can wish for him would be eternity.

Printed in *The Jackson Herald,* January 31, 2001

I SEE DAD EVERYWHERE

Why is it we don't fully appreciate the water until the well has gone dry? I took for granted all Dad's gestures of love until it was too late to show my appreciation.

Mementos from My Dad

Up until last week, I hadn't thought much about the reminders I have of Dad. I guess I was too busy thinking about Dad himself. After I found his shirt, I propped myself up in bed that night to read, but my mind kept wandering. Dad did woodwork until his hands became too arthritic and his mind confused. My thoughts settled first on the green wooden spoon holder he made that sits on my kitchen counter. Sturdy enough to last my lifetime, it will always hold my tableware.

A red heart candleholder Dad made years ago now sits on my dining table with other Valentine decorations. Today, I climbed up and down, painting a closet, on the sturdy folding wooden stool he made. Grandchildren used it for a unique kid-sized dining table until they outgrew it.

Before his retirement, Dad was a demolition expert, dismantling houses and businesses in several counties. When we first moved to Jackson County, he sold us an old Kelly Addition prefab for eight hundred dollars for a temporary home, paying employees three days wages to help move it to Jackson County.

Sick at the time, Dad helped us reconstruct the house without complaint. When we outgrew the four rooms, he offered us an old two-story house free of charge if we'd tear it down and transport it. Three years later, on our fourteenth wedding anniversary, we moved into our new home. We had bought used brick and other materials from Dad to complete the house. He helped roof it.

Dad gave us a maple four-poster bed with vanity and stool for our oldest daughter's bedroom and a bed with a ship's wheel for our son's, relics from his houses. "I know you'll make something out of these," he said. "I can't."

We sanded and stained Jackie's maple suite and painted Jim's red, white, and blue to match the nautical theme of his bedroom. Jackie had always wanted a canopy bed, so we converted the short posters of her bed to taller ones. A hand-carved maple leaf decorates the vanity front and bed's headboard. Once, when Dad was out for Christmas, we used the stool as an extra chair at the table. He noticed the joints were loose, took it home, and brought it back, solid as new.

Another time, Dad found an old oak upright piano in a house. Vandals (or a sorely frustrated pianist) had destroyed fourteen keys and five hammers. "I thought you might do something with it," Dad said. A piano tuner repaired the keys and hammers, and I stripped off green paint to reveal nice oak grain.

After several years, the piano wasn't worth tuning anymore. Jack bought me a beautiful antique concert grand. I wracked my brain for something to do with the intricately carved pieces of the old upright. An idea struck me. Why not a computer desk? Jack stripped the inner parts and lined the case with oak plywood. Drawers from an old treadle machine made disk compartments. Holes bored here and there directed wiring. A sliding mechanism and lid of the machine held the keyboard. A coat of polyurethane, and I was in business — literally. I've typed up many books and articles on my unique desk. It's quite a conversation piece, too.

I hadn't realized until today how many mementos of Dad surround my life. The shirt jolted me into sudden awareness of his sacrificial generosity and love. I deeply regret taking my father and his sacrifices for granted. If you still have yours with you, tell him today how much you love and appreciate him while you have time.

Printed in *The Jackson Herald,* February 7, 2001

I tried to show Dad my appreciation in small ways. During a vacation at Land of Canaan, he opens a sentimental birthday gift, a ceramic doll dressed like a farmer. Farming was so great a love of Dad's life that my husband Jack nicknamed him "Farmer Brown."

Ever Present

By sorrows in a prison cast,
Bound by chains of doubt,
My loving Savior met me there
And brought me safely out.

Beneath a burden buried deep,
A weight I could not bear,
My precious Lord proved his love,
Joining me in my despair.

In a valley dark, in death's shadows,
The path I could not see,
But I did not fear what lay ahead
For my Savior had gone before me.

Oh, God above, my God of love,
No matter where I am found,
I go not alone, for from your throne,
Your Son you have sent down.

A PREPARATION FOR WHAT IS TO COME

When Mom and I attended a friend's funeral together, I had no idea it was to be for me a trial run. By the weekend, we were planning Mom's funeral.

No Matter What, There's Always Hope

Mom and I attended a funeral today. A member of her church had died, a woman Jack and I worshipped with years ago at our home church in Charleston before moving to Jackson County. Viewing the woman's body, I couldn't help but think of Dad.

Before this, I felt it would be better to know if my father were dead or alive. Now I wasn't sure. As the family wept around the casket, I thought of how hard it would be to have to tell Dad goodbye, knowing it was the last time we would see him here on earth.

In the eulogy, the minister said, "You haven't lost anything if you know where it is. You know your loved one is in heaven, so you've not lost her; she's just gone on ahead."

This thought, intended to comfort the family, troubled me. We don't know where Dad is, so I guess we have really lost him.

Mom told me that my sister had learned that she could go to court and have Dad declared dead so Mom could begin drawing on his Social Security. Although Mom doesn't have much to live on, she said she wasn't ready for that yet. I know what she means. As I looked at that casket and thought about Dad, I found some comfort in not knowing, as all hope is not gone until you do know.

As the funeral songs were sung, I thought of how often Dad sang his favorite song, "Just a Closer Walk with Thee." I told someone, just after Dad disappeared, that if his body was found, that song should be sung at his funeral.

Mom told me that sometimes, as she and Dad walked through the field behind their house holding hands, he would sing, "Just a closer walk with Louise." She berated him for it, feeling it was blasphemous.

I understood Mom's feelings, but I also think Jesus understood Dad's feelings and didn't mind him substituting Mom's name for His at times. After all, Jesus knew Dad reverenced Him and God above all others, and he and Mom had held hands and walked down life's path together for sixty-four years, about the same length of time that they had both walked with Jesus.

On the way home from the funeral, Mom and I lunched at Gino's in Sissonville. She met a friend there who asked her about Dad. Mom told her we didn't know a thing, except that God was with Dad, wherever he was, dead or alive.

I felt ashamed of my earlier thoughts. Dad will never be lost, as long as he and Jesus walk together, which I'm sure is true either way. Hope is never gone with Christ.

Another thing the minister said that impressed me was the importance of a folded napkin. He said that a server knew you weren't finished as long as your napkin was folded by your plate or on your lap. When you crumpled it up and laid it down, you were through. He said that when the disciples found the tomb empty, the napkin that had covered Jesus' face was neatly folded and laid aside. That meant He wasn't through yet.

He was coming back some day to finish up. On that day, He'll bring Dad's dead body up from this old earth and give him a new one, or He'll bring him back in the clouds with Him to meet the saints in the air. Either way, we'll be reunited with Dad. So I'll just keep expecting to meet Dad someday. I know I'll not be disappointed, as long as I keep looking up.

Printed in *The Jackson Herald,* February 28, 2001

Dad's Favorite Song

"Just a closer walk with thee,"
(He shuffles slowly from room to room)
"Grant it , Jesus, is my plea."
(Slips outside in the gathering gloom)
"Daily walking close to thee,"
(Down the road and out of sight)
"Let it be, dear Lord, let it be."
(Disappears into the cold, dark night).

"Through this world of toils and snares,"
(Fights his way up the long, steep hill)
"If I falter, Lord, who cares?"
(Stumbles, rolls, lies so very still.)
"Who will all my burdens bear?"
(No one to help, life ebbs away,)
"None but thee, dear Lord, none but thee."
(But he's not forgotten how to pray)

"When this feeble life is o'er,"
(Autumn leaves drift softly down)
"And time for me shall be no more,"
(Blankets the slight form on the ground.)
"Lead me gently, safely o'er"
(Safe at home, his trials past)
"To that shore, dear Lord, to that shore."
(A closer walk with Jesus, at last.)

THE ROAD GETS ROUGHER

*Just when you think it can't get worse, you're proven wrong.
I came home from a writer's board meeting in February to
find my losses increased.*

A Good Set of Shocks

Many of you may know I have suffered another shock. My mother was discovered lying along the creek bank below her house February 24, buried February 28. She suffered a massive heart attack while throwing out paper for composting. If you read my column last week, you also know Mom and I shared our last time together in the same funeral home where her body lay this week. I believe God was in the arrangements, preparing me for my ordeal through the minister's message and Mom's comments.

Jack and I left Friday morning for Pennsylvania. My family knew the location of my writer's board meeting, but I neglected to inform them of our chosen motel. In spite of extreme efforts, they could not locate me. We arrived home on Sunday evening to find two distraught daughters waiting. When I saw their faces, I knew something bad had happened, but I didn't think of Mom. My mother was extremely self-sufficient and strong-willed. I thought she would outlive me.

I believe God absorbed a great deal of the shock by not allowing my children to find me. The news sent my heart into arrhythmia and pain. If I had known about Mom, the trip home may have been too stressful. He absorbed more of the awful shock when I heard my weeping daughters tell Jack, "Grandma Miller is dead." As I sat crying in the parked car, God whispered to me, "Now she won't have to go into a nursing home."

My brother had called me the night before we left, saying we should meet with Mom on my return to discuss that as a possible solution to her worsening mental condition. I knew

Mom would resist with everything in her, just as she resisted our invitations to live with us. I didn't want to do that to her. None of us did.

The third shock absorber was, *Mom won't have to worry about Dad anymore.* My last day with my mother, she talked constantly of Dad, worrying about whether he had enough to eat or if his hair needed cutting. She said she stayed up nights, praying, crying, and reading her Bible. During the days, prayer was a constant. She told me she was repeatedly thinking, *Oh, God! Oh, God! Oh, God!* Her grief broke my heart. Now her grieving had ended. Mine had doubled.

But so did the comfort. The fourth absorber was the sympathy and concern of family, friends, strangers, and funeral personnel. People who carry their own burdens, some so heavy I wonder how they have any strength left, dropped their load for a while to shoulder ours.

God dwells in heaven, but He visited me this week. I saw His compassion in the eyes of His people. I felt His gentle caress in extended helping hands. I saw His feet as His people hurried to our side, His ears as they patiently listened. I felt His lips touch my cheek in holy kisses of comfort. I leaned on His strong chest and cried as family and friends held me close in my grief. I heard His voice in condolences and read His love letters in cards and flowers. His heart beat with mine as I leaned on my husband's strong chest

A thought came to me in the funeral home as I observed God working through His people. I envisioned myself as an automobile traveling life's rough road. The strong shocks that took the jolts and smoothed my ride were installed by God. Without His Spirit, I would be jarred beyond endurance.

Our cars are important to us. Our lives and souls more so. Have you allowed God to install a good set of shock absorbers?

Printed in *The Jackson Herald,* March 7, 2001

Mom and I were friends. Although we sometimes disagreed,
we shared many moments, tears, and laughter together.

Death of a Friend

Black engine speeds into Life's station,
Roaring down a lonesome track.
You step aboard with trepidation,
Cast one longing, last look back.
In your hand a one-way ticket
(no need of luggage where you go)
The mournful train glides from the station,
Pulling out so dread and slow.
With outstretched hand I run beside you
In vain attempt to hold you here;
Death's whistle blows one last warning,
Piercing wail upon my ear.
With one last rattle now Death's engine
Disappears around Life's bend,
Leaving me here in Sorrow's station,
Bereft without you, dearest friend.
Here I must linger for a moment
Before returning to life's rush,
Lost in aching, yearning grieving
Amid the lonely station's hush.
I mourn my loss with your departure
To some unseen, distant place,
But take comfort in remembering
The benevolence of the Conductor's face,
The loving welcome that He gave you and,
How when He reached for your one-way ticket,
I saw the nailprints in his hand.

IN SPITE OF IT ALL, WE WILL SURVIVE

My parents are gone, but they left me a survival kit — faith in God and trust in His strength when I have none.

When My Mother and Father Forsake Me

My younger sister gave a eulogy at Mom's funeral. I wanted to, but was afraid I'd break down. My heart echoed Sheila's recital of Mom's sacrifices for us. Although she gave up much of her life to enhance ours, Mom wasn't good with physical affection. The only intimacy I recall was her holding my hand as a child when we crossed Charleston's streets.

Mom wasn't good with loving touches, but she was great with loving actions, like catching the bus to my house every washday when my doctor told me not to lift heavy loads during a difficult pregnancy. Mom was exceptionally good at lifting heavy loads.

Mom made strawberry shortcake from Dad's patch for my birthdays in my youth. After my hair turned gray, she still came trudging up my long driveway with her bowl of strawberries, Dad by her side, toting shortcakes and a gift from his garden. They didn't speak love in words, but shared it in many other ways.

Mom was like a chocolate-covered cherry (my favorite candy until I had to give up caffeine), hard on the outside, but soft and sweet on the inside. I miss those sweet morsels, but I miss Mom a lot more. If I had her back, I would tell her I loved her every time I saw her.

The day before Mom's funeral, I woke up wanting to pull the covers over my head and stay in bed, but I've learned there's a better way to deal with sorrow. I reached for my Bible and devotional book instead.

The recommend scripture was Habakkuk 3:17-19. Habakkuk is a journal of the prophet's burden for Israel. I carried my own burden and wanted comfort, not condemnation. I decided to read the designated verses, then turn to Psalms.

I never got to Psalms. My eyes fell on Habakkuk 3:16. It could have been a recording of my physical reaction upon hearing of Mom's death. *"When I heard, my belly trembled; my lips quivered at the voice: rottenness entered into my bones, and I trembled in myself, that I might rest in the day of trouble . . ."*

God gave that rest in the recommended reading. *"Although the fig tree shall not blossom, neither shall fruit be in the vines; the labor of the olive shall fail, and the fields shall yield no meat; the flock shall be cut off from the fold, and there shall be no herd in the stalls: Yet, I will rejoice in the Lord, I will joy in the God of my salvation. The Lord God is my strength, and he will make my feet like hind's feet, and he will make me to walk upon mine high places."*

There will be no more strawberries, no onions and lettuce or sweet potatoes, no opportunities to say, "I love you." Dad's strawberry bed and garden lay desolate, but my heart does not. Mom and Dad have been cut off from the fold, but are secure in the Shepherd's sheepfold.

I walked past my phone yesterday and could hear Mom saying, "What're you doing?" I'm missing you, Mom, and wondering about Dad. But you both taught me where my strength lies.

One memory my sister spoke about was when her boyfriend was killed. Mom gathered Sheila's long, lanky frame on her lap like a baby, rocking and crying with her until their grief was temporarily exhausted. Seven funerals this past two weeks of family and friends. So many grieving children. All you survivors, your real survival lies in Psalms 27:10, KJV: *"When my father and my mother forsake me, then the Lord will take me up."*

Printed in *The Jackson Herald,* March 14, 2001

GOOD MEMORIES CHASE THE SORROW

My survival kit includes restive moments and memories made down through the years. The respite soothes, but for now, the memories abrade. Sometimes, abrasion is needed for healing.

Thank God for All the Good Times

Jack and I recently spent three days at our Monroe County camp. I awoke one morning to the sound of geese honking. "The alarm just went off," I joked. I dozed off and awoke to find Jack reading. "Those geese need to install a snooze alarm," I complained. No sooner had I said it than the bicycle-horn honking began again. The goose and gander had swum downstream and were now on the way back up the creek that fronts our property. They always stop before our cabin to say hello.

I'm not kidding! They do! The year we bought the camp, Jack and Jim waded upstream to fish and caught sight of their nest. A few weeks later, Jack saw them floating downstream. "The geese are here!" he yelled. I ran outside, expecting them to fly away at the commotion, but they stopped before the camp, spreading their wings and honking. Three half-grown, fluffy yellow goslings followed in their wake. The proud Mama and Papa waded out onto the bank, parading their offspring to give us a good look, then continued downstream. Every year, the adults visit, honking to let us know they're there. We've never seen babies again.

One evening, just as dusk was settling in, I sighted a beaver. Jack ran to get the camera. As I eased down the bank, the beaver dipped and swam, showing off. He came to within ten feet of me, posing as he stripped a limb of bark. I've got photos as proof, but too dark to be any good.

Deer, blue heron, and muskrat also visit, but are more skittish. Turtles warm themselves on the trunk of one of our yard trees, uprooted by floodwaters and lying nearly submerged. They also sun on a nearby rock. Jack came upon a family of otter upstream one day, teaching little ones to fish. One day, several vultures settled in the road behind the camp. We often see them sunning in a nearby tree.

I awoke the first night in our camp with the scent of mouse in my nostrils and a warm breath on my face. This was one creature I could have done without! We found she had chewed a hole in the mattress and built a nest deep inside. I suppose she wondered who was sleeping in her bed, and on close inspection, thought it was someone to big to challenge. If only she knew! We burned the mattress.

The only things that frighten me more than mice are snakes. I saw a black snake crawling up the fireplace one day as Mom and I conversed, sitting opposite each other on two couches. I can't remember who got out the door first, but I at least took time to turn around and run. Mom went out sideways, hopping like a kangaroo.

Our screams brought Jack running to kill the snake. Company came that night, but we kept our secret. I wondered how I would sleep, but we stayed up so late having fun, I could have slept with a copperhead as my bedfellow and not cared. I did get up once to make sure no snake was curled up with my infant grandson. We've snake-proofed the place since (we hope!).

We've had some great times at that camp with Mom and Dad. Mom died four days before we planned to take her again. I wish we could have had that one last time, but I guess I would never be satisfied. I just need to thank God for all the fun times and look forward to that heavenly reunion where snakes are harmless and good times never cease.

Printed in *The Jackson Herald,* April 11, 2001

THE WINTER HAS BEEN LONG AND HARD

Sometimes it seems our emotional winters last forever. For the sake of not only ourselves, but of others, it's time for a thaw, time once again for the flowering of hope.

For, Lo, the Winter Is Past

"For, lo, the winter is past, the rain is over and gone; The flowers appear on the earth; the time of the singing of birds is come, and the voice of the turtle{dove} is heard in our land;" Song of Solomon 2:11 &12 KJV

Darkness covered the land. Jesus gave up the ghost. The sorrowing disciples took Him from the cross, burying their dreams of Israel's peace with Him. A winter of emotions roiled in their souls. Despair shattered their hope.

But the sun arose, and before it, the Son in all His glory. An angel rolled the stone away, not that Jesus could depart the tomb, but that an unbelieving and brokenhearted Peter could look inside, know His Savior had risen, and once again enter the door of belief.

I have endured a winter of despair, beginning years before the day I stood weeping at my mother's tomb. The first chilling drop of rain fell when my parents visited and my father didn't know the way home. The rain continued to fall, icy, driven sheets assaulting my heart and emotions. I stood in the elements, drenched with grief, watching my parents succumb to senility and helplessness. Observing their struggle to retain what slowly slipped away, my grief deepened.

Some lose their loved ones in an instant. I'm not denying their grief. I know it is just as deep, just as real. But I watched my mother and father die inch by inch until the only thing left was what God gave — a hope of heaven.

God rolled back my heavy stone of despair one day this week and allowed me a look inside. He showed me that nature's beauty is stunted by the first blast of wintry air, soon halted altogether. Earth lies barren, limbs stripped of growth and flowers denuded. *Your pessimism,* He whispered, *has unfortunately stopped your spiritual growth, and perhaps slowed the growth of others, but hope is not gone.*

Just as Jesus arose from the dead, just as the disciples hope was restored, what your pessimism has destroyed, Sonlight can cause to grow again. You need only realize that hope is alive, to lift your hands and heart toward Heaven in praise, to raise your eyes and see Jesus, risen and standing on my right hand in your defense. Hope is not gone. It is alive and well. You need only to stop doubting and believe.

Dry your tears and look outside, God said. *Winter is past. Chilling rains have fallen, but the sun shines again. The earth has greened, flowers have resurrected, bursting overnight into glorious bloom.*

God revealed that my dark clouds not only hamper my sunshine, but my chilling winds of discouragement hover over loved ones, blocking out their light. I have carried about these clouds of depression long enough. The time has come to allow the mighty wind of the Holy Spirit to drive them away, to allow warm rays of His love to shine through.

It sometimes takes time for clouds to pass, for flowers to grow. It will take time for my skies to brighten, for my heart to bloom again. But I am determined that I not darken other's lives any longer. Hope overcomes sorrow. I would forever dwell in dark, barren winters without this hope that begins in my Risen Lord.

Printed in *The Jackson Herald,* April 18, 2001

WINTER'S CHILLING BLAST RETURNS

Just when I expected a thaw, another storm hit, this one chilling to the bone. Yet I had learned to brave the elements. And when the hard winds blow, shelter is near.

I've Had More Than My Share

By the time you read this, my father's remains will rest beside my mother's in the Floral Hills Garden of Memories. As with my mother, I was away when my father was found, spending what we had hoped to be three fun days at camp with grandchildren. We had a bad beginning, with eight-year-old Josh virus-sick on the way, two more sick the next day, and one falling while fishing, waterproof waders overflowing with Second Creek's chilling, spring-fed stream.

"I hope tomorrow proves better than today," I remember remarking. That's when the phone call came. Since my father's disappearance over six months ago, I imagined experiencing great relief when he was found. What I felt was as if a truckload of stones had been dumped inside me. Dad's body was discovered caught beneath a barbed wire fence within sight of home. "Where he was, he could see the top of his house," a neighbor said.

So many people volunteered to do a community search, but officials disallowed it, saying we would confuse the dogs on picking up Dad's scent or someone else might get lost. We sat in the house, awake all night, not allowed out, while my Dad wandered perhaps most of the time within shouting distance of home. If we had been allowed to search then, would we have found him?

I don't know. I do know officials went beyond the call of duty. Why Dad wasn't found, why dogs' reactions and eyewitnesses pointed him traveling in the opposite direction than his body was discovered, I don't know. My youngest sister reminds me, "If Dad had returned that night, would the spiritual change have come about in Mom?" Probably not. Would we children have drawn closer together?

Yet why should Dad have to suffer for our sins, he who strove to live above sin? We could ask ourselves the same question of Christ. I suppose the answer is in Apostle Paul's words in Romans 8:18 KJV: *"For . . . the sufferings of this present time are not worthy to be compared with the glory which shall be revealed in us."*

We measure sufferings according to our life span. God measures them by eternity, an immeasurable difference. If temporal earthly sufferings increase eternal glory, isn't it worth the enduring? Cures for many diseases are painful, yet profitable enough to warrant severe temporary suffering: surgeries, chemotherapy, physical therapy, wound abrasion, etc.. The cure for earthly foibles seems as necessary for eternal well being. This reaches my mind right now. It will take a while to reach my heart.

Being away from home with four children was a blessing. If you've never heard a granddaughter's soft, sympathetic, "Grandma?" when she hears you crying in your room, the sweet consolation as her arms go around your neck, her holding you close while she whispers comforting words, I can't explain the feeling. I know it will remain a cherished memory until death or senility erases it. Not even the youngest complained about aborting our trip. I felt their love. That's what it takes to get us through these earthly sufferings, God's love, human love.

"You've had your share of suffering lately," some say. Yes, but I've also had more than my share of love. Aren't you glad love can't be depleted? That's another one of God's "immeasurables."

Printed in *The Jackson Herald,* April 25, 2001

REAPING MOM AND DAD'S INHERITANCE

My parents' lived fairly frugal lives, but I was surprised to find they left us a vast inheritance, riches beyond compare. In return, they were now receiving a great return on their life investments.

Cashing in on a Savings Plan

"Lay not up for yourselves treasures upon earth, . . . but lay up for yourselves treasures in heaven . . . ." Matthew 6: 19, 20 KJV

My father's funeral was Friday. We had scheduled it earlier, but had to cancel until authorities positively identified Dad's remains. The cancellation was a knife thrust in a raw wound. We did all we could to notify those who might respond. I don't know if anyone showed up at the funeral home {we learned later that some did}, but flowers had been ordered, work schedules changed, out-of-state family notified.

Before the discovery of Dad's body, Mom's estate auction had been planned to cover funeral expenses, as neither had life insurance. Already advertised, we had no choice but to proceed. The knife was twisted. Not that anyone was pursuing payment, but Mom and Dad taught us debts should be paid promptly, if at all possible and however inconvenient.

When Dad was drafted into the Navy in World War II, as soon as Mom received the monthly check, we walked to the grocery store a good distance away to settle the account. To me it was an opportunity to share that free bag of candy with my siblings. I'm sure Mom saw it differently.

Mom was always a stickler about debt. She told me once about owing on a cookstove she and Dad bought when they set up housekeeping. She rode the bus to town one day and, after paying bills, had less than a dollar left. She walked into the hardware and handed the dealer those last few coins. She felt foolish when he laughed at her. She laughed when she told me, but I didn't laugh. I felt proud.

Years ago, I borrowed a loaf of bread. When I paid Mom for it, she shocked me by saying, "You forgot the tax." Dad sold us a load of used brick from his demolition business and, being his child, I supposed (wrongly) that he would give us a discount. But Mom and Dad weren't selfish. They were teaching accountability.

Mom and Dad weren't always so exact in financial matters. They shared war ration coupons with store customers in the aftermath of World War II and gave selflessly of time and money to five married children with their own finances in short supply. Mom accompanied me to town when our home mortgage was in arrears, walking from finance agency to finance agency, seeking a loan to rescue us from foreclosure.

My parents were good at rescuing their children from trouble. They died without savings, withdrawing most of it as loans to save other children from financial disaster. Did I say Mom and Dad didn't have any savings? Let me reword that. Mom and Dad were rich. They had treasures stored in heaven, gathering interest for years. If they had millions banked down here, what good would it do them now? Now they're cashing in on that heavenly account that, unlike earthly savings, can't be depleted.

Yes, Mom and Dad were sticklers when it came to debts. They felt they owed a lot to the Lord. Over the years, they repaid a little here, a little there. But I believe both accounts have now been marked "Paid In Full."

Printed in *The Jackson Herald,* May 2, 2001

Living Proof

His shoulders weren't broad,
But they had enough room to cry on.
He wasn't a wealthy man,
But we could count on his last dollar,
If we needed it.
He was almost handsome,
But he had funny ears.
He always said they made him look like a car
Coming down the road with both doors open,
But he never failed to listen when we talked.
Arthritis twisted his hands,
But not until he couldn't give us
An encouraging pat on the back
When we were down
Or a handshake
When congratulations were in order.
His feet were small for a man,
But no one else could ever fill his shoes.
My dad wasn't a tall man,
But he stood taller in my eyes
Than any man I know.
No, my father wasn't a perfect man,
But he would be the first to admit it,
And he wouldn't want me to say he was,
Since he taught me to never lie.
He always worked hard,
Holding down as many as three jobs
In order to supply our needs.
He didn't worry much about our wants.
We had to work to get those ourselves.
He always said hard work and doing without
Built character—
And then he lived to prove it.

GOD SENDS HIS LOVE

Sometimes, in dark times, we lose sight of God. We know He exists, but we can't reach out and touch Him. But if we call out, He assures us He is near.

God, Are You There? His Answer: "Yes!"

Some prayers seem to go unanswered. Many said of Dad, "So many are praying for your father's discovery. Why doesn't God answer?" I don't know. I can only say I'm grateful Dad wasn't found while Mom was still alive or that Dad was there to witness Mom's death. I can't imagine either suffering the knowledge of where and how each died.

But couldn't God have prevented their deaths? He could have. But perhaps both suffered more through living. That provokes another question; couldn't God have healed their senility and diseases? Dwelling on doubt thoroughly tests faith. But I've learned faith is believing when there seems no reason to believe.

My son asked me once, "Mom, what does it really mean to be a Christian?" My reply was, after careful consideration, "Serving God and wholly believing, even if He slays you." I still say the same. We either believe or we don't. It's that simple. I choose to believe.

I've experienced miraculous answers to prayer; I've also had times when God seemed distant and silent. I sat in church after Mom died, grieving while others rejoiced. *God, I need to feel your arms around me,* I prayed. A still small voice spoke to my heart, *You just did.* My husband had minutes before put a comforting arm around me when he sensed my distress.

God, I need to hear You speak my name, I persisted. Another reply, *You just did.* My name had echoed around the church during family prayer, heartfelt petition for my comfort. I found that comfort in the service.

There's a new version of "The Footprints of God", two sets of footprints, one steady and straight, the other erratic, reminding me of times I wavered like the wind, trusting, then doubting, walking close by God's side, then wandering away. Suddenly, big footprints swallow the small ones. That's when I learned to trust God, walking in His footsteps, no matter where they lead. Then, suddenly, both footprints circle crazily.

That's the time we danced, God tells me. God and I danced this week. Fearful of more tragedy, I requested prayer for another camp getaway. A warm sun bathed our entire week. Young emerald leaves waved in fresh spring breezes. A black bear foraged within sight. Mama and Papa geese floated past, circling and honking, introducing three golden goslings. A mink carrying her baby swam past Jack as he fished. Wild turkey, squirrels, chipmunks, and rabbits abounded.

A flock of yellow Swallowtail butterflies inhabited our millrace for two days, their choreography mesmerizing as they soared around us. I believe God was the Choreographer. On an evening walk to huge rocks, Jack and I observed geese bathing in shallow rapids. Unafraid, they conversed with us until we left. Yes, God, along with His creation, danced with Jack and me on our belated anniversary celebration.

Jack wanted to take me to town to buy me a special gift. I had already received one. Maybe what I said in my column last week about our anniversary explains our love affair with God. A mature love needs neither frills nor celebration. It is a daily celebration. Yet, sometimes God gives special gifts to prove His love. He sent Jack and me one this week. Thank you, God. You proved you are there.

Printed in *The Jackson Herald,* May 16, 2001

DON'T BORROW SORROW

Sometimes we look ahead, dreading the future. Then the future arrives and we find our fears were foolish, that the dreaded foe is a welcome friend.

Mother's Day Has Come and Gone

"Her children arise up, and call her blessed ."
Proverbs 31:28 KJV

Mother's Day has come and gone, but memories linger on. I have to admit I dreaded Mother's Day. With Mom gone, how could I get through the celebration? But awakening on Sunday morning, I looked over at the collage of photos in the frame on my dresser that my oldest daughter Jackie had given me for Christmas. In one photo, Mom and Dad pressed cheek to cheek during their fiftieth wedding anniversary, big smiles on their faces. A peace swept over me. Mom had little to smile about after Dad's disappearance, but with her passing, her burden had passed.

The day created more cherished memories for me. Jackie called before Sunday School, wishing me a happy Mother's Day and telling me she loved me, although she had come on a special visit on Friday. I know, in her heart, she yearned to ease my sadness.

The middle daughter Kim came after Sunday School with her family, bringing me a bright red geranium, cards, kisses, and hugs. We spent the afternoon together buying more flowers, then stopped at Kim's long enough for Pappaw, Stone, and Teagan to fight a water battle. The third daughter Debbie had presented me the day before with an elegant lily and a meal at her house.

On the way home from Kim's, we stopped at our son Jim's house to learn the results of Saturday's fishing tournament. "We were just coming to see you," he said. He handed me a white package gilded with a royal purple ribbon and a card. His wife Terri handed me a gift bag. "This one is from me," she emphasized. I am not one to easily weep, but I felt tears surge to the surface when I pulled out a framed print that said, "If mothers were flowers, I would pick you." This silent message meant so much.

The other package held a beautiful wind chime with a cardinal etched in the glass weight. Each time I hear the chime, I hear notes of love. Each time I see the flowers from my daughters, I am reminded that love grows with tender care. Each time my eyes fall upon the framed print, I thank God for a daughter-in-law who, in her quiet way, has lifted burdens and brought peace and joy to her home and ours.

. But Mother's Day brought two more precious gifts. My daughter Kim's tests proved, "No cancer." My son told us on our visit, "Sorry, Mom and Dad, I love you, but I've got to get ready for church." How many times had we yearned to hear that? In the past, we had often driven by his house with a heavy heart and a prayer for his salvation.

One Wednesday night after church, he called. "Mom, can you and Dad come down? I have something to tell you." I feared the worst until I heard his laughter. Then I knew. We dropped everything and hurried down. The "happy hour" we shared only God could give. He had won my son at last. I don't deserve such blessings, but I sure did bask in them this Mother's Day.

Printed in *The Jackson Herald,* May 23, 2001

A PART OF MOM LIVES ON

When loved ones die, they live on through children and grandchildren. On my first birthday, after Mom and Dad's death, I found that out in a special way.

STRAWBERRIES CAN MAKE YOU CRY

My mother is gone, but tradition lives on. In the past, my youngest daughter Debbie has surprised me with a scrumptious birthday cake filled with whipped cream and drenched in luscious ripe, red, strawberries.

This year, my middle daughter Kim and her husband Fred, along with grandchildren, Teagan and Stone, brought lots of wonderful gifts. The one that topped them all was slices of angel food cake, a can of whipped cream, and a bowl of sweetened strawberries. There had to be forethought in adding gifts of clothing a little too large.

"I wanted to carry on Grandma Miller's tradition," Kim said. "I never put sugar on my strawberries, but I knew Grandma did. I wanted to do it as much like hers as I could. Did she make strawberry shortcake?"

"No, a one-egg cake," I replied. "And she mashed the berries a little."

"Then that's what I'll do next year," Kim said. As we talked afterwards, my oldest daughter called from Ohio, singing "Happy Birthday!" over the phone. She promised to see me over the weekend. I wonder if she will come up my driveway with strawberry shortcake.

I received a card from my oldest sister Eleanor the next day. "If I could be with you on your birthday," she wrote, "I would make you a one-egg cake and serve it with strawberries.

But Cracker Barrel has a delicious strawberry shortcake, so have Jack take you out and enjoy!"

The card was signed, Love, Doodie (the nickname Dad gave her when rocking her as a baby, "my little doodlebug") & Dave. She didn't have to add the love. I felt it in the remembrance of the tradition, the desire to carry it on, and the twenty-dollar bill she enclosed to pay for the shortcake. The card will go into my cedar chest with all my others, watermarked with a few tearstains.

Mom's tradition is not all that lives on. She lives on, too. She left a little of herself in all of us. She still hugs me through my daughters. She makes me smile through my sisters (and sometimes weep). She trudges up memory lane with that special bowl of strawberries and one-egg cake through loved ones carrying on tradition. And she lives on in my heart, moving in sixty years ago and claiming squatter's rights. I couldn't dispossess her if I wanted to, and I don't.

When Kim asked for Mom's recipe, I left out the first few ingredients. "Build a huge, above-ground strawberry bed that allows a woman with a bad back to pick without stooping. Keep alert, with an old two-barrel shotgun, for predators of deer and groundhog. Spend days weeding and cultivating (a father must do all the above). Spend hours in the hot sun picking fruit, more hours cleaning it. Slice in a bowl big enough to allow four hungry grandchildren and a son-in-law to share the gift (a mother's contribution). Divide and eat, laughing a lot (everyone!). Note: The one-egg cake actually takes a half dozen to bake enough to go around. That's the best recipe of love I have ever read — or devoured!

Printed in *The Jackson Herald*, June 6, 2001

A FRACTURED FAMILY MENDS

When our extended family found it difficult to personally share Christmas, my oldest sister suggested we celebrate in July. Our "Christmas in July" celebration this particular year surprisingly centered around me.

Christmas in July

Our "Christmas in July" Miller family reunion was held June 30th at our daughter Kim's house. We began these gatherings because our extended family became too widespread and busy at Christmas to get together. We don't exchange gifts at these summer get-togethers, but we do exchange a lot of fun and laughter.

Before we left the house, I thought of how, in previous years, we picked Mom and Dad up and took them with us. On the way, they sat in the back seat, Mom talking a mile a minute and Dad listening. Dad wasn't as vocal as Mom, occasionally making a comment. Mom, like me, was never at a loss for words.

Last year, Mom and Dad wore paper crowns — our beloved king and queen, reigning for the day. As Dad offered grace before the meal, I sneaked a peek and took his picture. "I didn't mean to be irreverent," I told my sister-in-law, "but Dad may not be here next year." Three months later, Dad was missing.

With the family fractured, not in camaraderie and spirit, but as a unit, things weren't quite the same. But the food was great, as usual. Dad's flag, presented at his military funeral, hung by the porch. Jack was given the privilege of offering prayer. After we filled our plates, Kim made an announcement. Knowing she intended to hold the reunion at a park in the future, I expected that. What I got was, "This is a surprise sixtieth birthday celebration for Mom."

Since my birthday had been May 29th, I was totally surprised. I received nice gifts and cards. The day nearly over, we lounged around with sated appetites. Teagan asked me to play badminton. With the heat, humidity, and a full tummy, I could barely breathe, much less run. "I can't, honey," I said. "I'm too tired." Her disappointment made me reconsider. "I tell you what," I said. "I'll play, but if you don't get the birdies within reach, you have to chase them."

It wasn't long until Kim, niece Nikki, and grandson Casey joined us. When Casey left, Kim's husband Fred and my oldest sister Eleanor took over. Others gathered to watch, a senior citizen cheering squad. We had a lot of fun, and I felt better afterwards — even though I did a lot of chasing. Sometimes it takes a little extra activity to get the old heart pumping.

Spiritual families are the same. We need to get up and get going, to gather with Christian brothers and sisters, giving out gifts of love, sating our spiritual appetites at God's table. We need to run for the Lord and form cheerleading squads of encouragement for others.

We needn't set aside a special day to celebrate spiritual independence. Christ became a part of the human family, wore the crown of thorns, and took our place on the cross so that we could celebrate spiritual freedom every day. What a precious gift! We never know who might be missing from our spiritual family next year, but one day there will be a great big family reunion, a celebration of new births without end. I hope you don't miss it.

Printed in The Jackson Herald, July 11, 2001

KING AND QUEEN FOR A DAY

MEMORIES ARE MADE OF THIS

One day, making my bed, I arranged my handcrafted pillows on it (two photo pillows from my daughter Jackie, an embroidered one from my late friend Dorothy, and a crocheted one from my granddaughter Danielle). I began to think of all the memorabilia Jack and I have in our home, and how these loving gifts transform a sterile house into a cozy and comfortable dwelling.

Experiencing the Memory Curve

In May of 1959, Jack and I began our marriage in a tiny three-bedroom house on Rich Fork of Kanawha Two Mile, just outside of Charleston. New and devoid of memories, our little house soon became a home. Old friends visited, new ones were made, and four children were born in the seven years we lived there.

Selling the house and moving proved an exciting but wrenching adventure. We told friends goodbye and uprooted our children from their beginnings. Today, thirty-five years later, I still see sunlight playing on the wooden floors and hear the children splashing in the bath.

After a year of living in an old rented house without a bath on Angel Ridge in Fairplain of Jackson County, we built a temporary four-room abode on Winters Road, off of Grasslick. Outgrowing this old restructured prefab, we then built the house we now occupy.

It didn't take long to fill our new home with memories, but they were created on a curve. Memories in the first home were made of beginnings, many here of endings. The children matured, married, and moved away, and many of our friends have passed on.

Dorothy Jackson's beautifully embroidered pillow decorates my wicker bedroom chair, her blue porcelain candleholder my coffee table, and her cutwork sheets my guest bed. A good writer friend, Dorothy passed her writings to me when she died. I treasure them and will never dispose of them.

The dresser Jack and I purchased before our marriage is still in use, a memory too fond to discard. We laid away the bedroom suite when I was fifteen. When my parents refused to let us marry, the company stored the suite for two years. The dresser, the only thing from those early years, besides our marriage, that survived, holds a multi-photo frame displaying pictures of our deceased parents.

Two pillows, crafted by Jackie, display photos of Jack's family, only three of six still living. A snapshot of Denver Koontz, Jack's deceased friend, sits on his bedside table, one of James Marion, Jackie's boyfriend and precious to us, in our family room. James drowned at seventeen.

A decorative plate from Jack's deceased Aunt Belle hangs on our kitchen wall. A goblet from "Uncle Dan", a past member of our church, and six long-stemmed goblets from Jack' s departed sister, Joann, fill a shelf in the kitchen. Mom's cookie jar I bought at sixteen and the old hand-operated meat slicer from our little country store sit atop a cabinet. Dad's handmade stool is used to reach my hanging flowers and his tableware holder sits on my counter.

Two candy dishes we gave my Grandmother Nickell on the first Christmas of our marriage are stored in the hutch purchased from Jack's Aunt Sadie, who now resides in Elder Care. The card Grandmother Nickell sent on my fourth birthday (marked with bathwater stains) is in my cedar chest. Jack rests in Mom's recliner, and guests sleep in my childhood bed, under Mom's beautiful poppy quilt.

Memories. Our first were made of beginnings, more recently, endings. Yet the keepsakes, although sometimes saddening, create a warm atmosphere of treasured times with loved ones. We are surrounded by a great cloud of witnesses proclaiming that although loved ones die, love does not. Love lives on forever.

Printed in *The Jackson Herald* August 22, 2001
Reprinted as "Love Lives on Forever" February 13, 2002

Mom and Dad made a lot of memories in their Derrick's Creek home. I understood their reluctance to leave it.

WE DO NOT SUFFER ALONE

Suffering is not exclusively ours. Not one soul on earth will ever get through this life without suffering, but leaning on one another props us up when Satan tries to topple us. Leaning on God rests us until strength returns.

I Remember, Weep, and Pray

A son who has lost his mother asks, "How can I face my future without my future by my side?" A teen says of her lost fiancé, "He was a wonderful man." A firefighter wonders, "Why my co-workers and not me?" Hearts are touched as mourners tell stories of loved ones lost in the September 11 terrorists' attacks. "What I feel in my mind can't compare with what I feel in my heart," another firefighter reveals.

How can we explain emotions evoked by such heartbreaking stories? A father-to-be, on the way home for the birth of his baby, is cheated of fatherhood by a fatal plane crash. A mother, who traded her dangerous career as a policewoman for the "safer" one of an airline attendant, joins others in death. Two close friends, planning a trip together, are forced to take separate planes, one flying into the North Tower, the other into the South.

"We feel their pain, because we've been there," Oprah Winfrey says. And she's right. When I see the flags flying, I remember the veteran's flag that covered Dad's casket. When I see fliers held by hopeful family members, I recall bulletins posted across the country in hopes someone would have news of Dad. When a weeping wife tells of how she smells her husband everywhere, I think of how, when I least expect it, I catch Mom's special scent, feel her warm flesh against mine.

I hear Dad's gentle voice, his soft sigh, feel the soft stubble of his beard against my face. And I feel so bereft. Memories are bittersweet. We cherish them, but they are no substitute for real flesh and blood.

"It's strange, when I should be grieving," a mourner remarked, "but I can feel a change in the air. These lives were not lost in vain." And she's right. Lackadaisical worshippers are alive with new enthusiasm, empty hearts are turning to God. Our nation is experiencing a spiritual revival that could turn the world upside down. Only through these happenings can we make sense of the immense losses.

When I try to make sense of my tragedy, I think of how Dad's disappearance brought family unity to children fractured by stress, how Mom grew closer to God and more loving to others, how people reached out and touched us, forever changing hearts.

Paul tells believers in II Corinthians 4:6 KJV, "*For God, who commanded the light to shine out of darkness, hath shined in our hearts, to give the light of the knowledge of the glory of God in the face of Jesus Christ.*" God not only created the sun, the moon, and the stars to penetrate earth's darkness, His love for mankind shone brightest in the darkest hours ever known on this earth, the day Jesus gave His life that we might have life everlasting. Without hope in His resurrection, how could we endure?

God also causes the light of His love to shine out of the hearts of men, piercing tribulation's darkness. Paul asked, in Hebrews 13:3 KJV, *"Remember them that are in bonds, as bound with them, and them which suffer adversity, as being yourselves also in the body."* I remember, weep, and pray.

Printed in *The Jackson Herald,* October 3, 2001

AUTUMN WILL NEVER SEEM THE SAME

Dad's disappearance on a bitterly cold October evening, his consequent death, and later discovery changed forever my conception of fallen leaves.

Lady Bugs and Fallen Leaves

I spend much of my time these days sweeping up ladybugs and watching the swirl of autumn leaves. You never know what will set off a memory of departed loved ones. With Mom, it is a ringing telephone, canning, and crocheted afghans. With Dad, it is ladybugs, gardens, and fallen leaves. While we spent days at Mom's, waiting and watching for news of Dad, ladybugs swarmed the place. Some days people had to battle their way to the door. To remain outside was to be bombarded and bitten by the little orange bombers.

Not able to remain idle after my return home those uncertain days after October 8th, 2000, I helped Jack paint the house. This may seem uncaring to many, but he needed help, and I just couldn't sit still. Activity kept my mind off my worry and grief. I swept ladybugs from Jack's back and picked them out of the fresh paint. Now every time I sweep up ladybugs, I recall the horror of those days.

When Dad's body was found, we learned he was covered with fallen leaves the same color as his clothes, which made him almost invisible. I couldn't help but think of how my four-year-old grandson prayed for God to bring a warm blanket to put over Grandpa Miller. I pictured a caring God observing Dad's fall, His gentle breath stirring the trees above him, a rustling of sunwarmed leaves swirling down and blanketing his chilled body.

After Dad's disappearance, I walked a country road with Jack. A single miniature gold-and-lime leaf fell, swirling to the ground at my feet. Jack unaware, I was the only one, other than God, who witnessed its fall. I wrote a metaphoric poem about Dad, of how the world spun on like a carousel and the sun continued to shine, unaware my father was gone. I never see a leaf fall but what I think of Dad. Climbing into the car one day, I noticed a miniature leaf, a replica of the one that came to rest at my feet, lying on the threshold of the door. I gently brushed it out onto the sidewalk. I really wanted to pick it up and carry it home.

Fallen leaves and chilled autumn days forecast winter's approach and the year's end. The remaining tomatoes on the vine make me think of Mom. In her good years, she never let a garden fruit go to waste. I think of her as I pick up my yarn to crochet, now that the days are cooler. She made afghans for all the grandchildren on their graduations. I think of her as the deer eat the strawberry plants in our patch.

Fallen leaves and ladybugs make me think of the horror of those days and Dad's tragic death, but they also make me think of his life and destination. Just as the ladybugs seek warmth and the year goes out in a blaze of glory, I'm sure Dad did the same. The cold may have preceded his entrance into the haven of rest, but the Light of the Son would have dispelled the chill before his feet hardly touched those streets of gold.

Printed in *The Jackson Herald, October 31, 2001*

GOD RESTORES WHAT SATAN HAS STOLEN

Job suffered much, yet God was with him through it all and restored his happiness. He is doing the same for me.

Now I Know How Job Felt

As you read this, Thanksgiving is a week past, but I am writing this Thanksgiving night. I usually write my columns on Monday to submit on Friday for Wednesday's publication, but I wanted to wait and see what blessings Thanksgiving wrought.

With Mom and Dad gone and my oldest daughter separated from her husband, I figured the count was down at least three. My youngest daughter Debbie called Monday, telling me her husband was in the emergency room and might be admitted to the hospital. If she and my grandson Matthew spent the day there with him, that could eliminate three more.

My son Jim had to work, the older grandchildren are always busy, and Teagan and Stone had dental surgery yesterday. Things didn't look promising, but just in case (wishful thinking), I bought two sixteen-pound turkeys and thirty-six rolls and declared another war on ladybugs and attic flies. I shooed away dustbunnies, who, with squatter's rights, would surely return. The ladybugs refuse to be ousted.

As Job mourned his losses, then recouped, I have much to be thankful for. Granddaughter Danielle, her friend Mark, and Josh and Kendra came yesterday, attending prayer meeting with us. After church I baked a cake, then gave Mark a crash course in piano theory. He left a good while after midnight. We got to bed after one. I dreamed of Mom and Dad all night, not good dreams.

But Debbie's husband didn't have to be hospitalized. Papa and Matthew hunted a little before dinner. By the time I had mopped the kitchen, cleaned the bathroom, and took a shower, the turkey was golden brown and family had begun pouring in. Eighteen is slightly off our former tally, but I'm thankful for those who were here, all the kids except my son, and not a grandchild missing out of ten. From the ages of four to twenty, they are a beautiful, intelligent bunch.

Now the house is nearly silent. A clock ticks, my computer hums, and Jack's TV is a distant sound. Ladybugs are creeping out of their hiding places, and the dustbunnies are reclaiming their territory. Life resumes normal rhythm, like white-water-rafting into a placid stream after plunging through exciting currents.

I have been reminded much today of sorrows family members have borne and are bearing, some battling diseases and others emotional pain. I have thought much of the losses terrorism has caused and the terror of Afghanistan wars. My heart goes out to those caught in whirlpools of despair. I pray that God will give my family peace and sweet victory in the days ahead, and may He grant better days to each of the mourners of the September 11th tragedy and beyond, and to our soldiers, and refugees of war.

I have fought my own wars and suffered my own losses, but like Job, God always restores what Satan steals away. God has allowed me pleasant memories and sweet victories. For this, I say, *"Bless the Lord, O my soul: and all that is within me, bless his holy name. Bless the Lord, O my soul, and forget not all his benefits."* Psalm 103:1 &2 KJV

Printed in *The Jackson Herald,* November 28, 2001

THE ONLY WAY OUT IS UP

Growing old is sometimes a depressing venture into deep valleys, but it is good to know that just over the horizon, our rock-strewn path ends and our strength is restored. Like an eagle, we will spread our wings and fly into the bosom of God.

Joy Comes in the Morning

Jack and I visited two Eldercare residents several Sundays ago. I'm not bragging, because we felt ashamed we hadn't gone earlier. We followed up with a visit to another good friend, homebound and dying with liver cancer.

Although we usually receive blessings from these visits, depression settled in. I couldn't keep from thinking of Mom and Dad and their vehement objections to nursing home care. Although I never entertained the thought, I now better realized why they didn't want to go. It was a place of sadness.

In spite of excellent care, those we visited yearned for home. I lost all ambiguity about whether we should have placed Dad in a home to avoid his tragic end. I am glad we allowed Mom and Dad to live out their last days walking the fields they loved, sitting on the bench by their small stream, watching sunshine and shadow play on fish and fallen leaves.

I'm thankful they had a few more days to sit in their walled-in back porch, observing birds feed and squirrels poach from the variety of feeders Dad constructed and hung from tree limb, yard swings, and posts. I'm glad they spent their last days puttering about the house, surrounded by lifetime memories.

Of course, I realize some situations and health-needs demand nursing home care, but I'm thankful Mom and Dad remained fairly strong and self-reliant until the end, able to manage with occasional help.

"Lord," I asked, as we walked toward our car, "why does life have to end like this, with so much misery and pain? Why can't we just live healthy and happy until you call us home?" Our next visit was with Clarence Campbell, a man who timbered with Jack years ago.

Although near death and bedfast, Clarence had a big smile and a few humorous stories to tell. In his situation, his cheerful personality was surprising and immensely uplifting. He had told his wife the night before, "The Lord is coming for me tonight." He was ready to go, but his trip was delayed for a few days, perhaps for our sakes. Not only did we get to see him one more time, but also our visit with him lifted my lingering depression.

That night in church, a thought came to me. A pregnant woman becomes really miserable as the end of her pregnancy nears, but she anticipates the birth, although aware it will be painful. The baby arrives and all suffering is forgotten, or at least forgiven. These dear friends of ours are noticeably miserable in a physical sense, but each speaks often of the Lord, anticipating relief from frailties of old age. When we depart this world and are born anew in God's kingdom, all the miseries of aging will be forgotten. Joy will replace sorrow and tears.

None of us knows what waits in declining years, but we can know that, after we reach the bottom of the decline, the only good way out is up. I talked with a friend this weekend whose husband had died of cancer without hope of eternity. "He was so afraid," she said. "So afraid." I wish he had known the remedy to fear. I'm glad Mom and Dad did.

THE SUN POPS OUT FROM BEHIND DARK CLOUDS

When dark clouds hover or nights seem dark and long, it is good to remember that clouds are temporary, the sun is permanent. Behind heavy clouds, the sun still shines and will soon reappear. Long nights pass and day breaks as the perpetual sun chases away shadows.

Sometimes You Get a Double Whammy

Since the year 2000, Jack and I have driven to Beaver Falls, Pennsylvania, twice a year, in February and September, combining writers' board meetings at Geneva College with a two-day vacation. These vacations were spoiled for me last year in two ways. In February, my mother died while I was away. In September, the meeting fell on the weekend after the tragic terrorist's attack.

Have you heard of persons suffering depression before learning of a loved one's death? A cloud of depression hung over me during our February trip last year. My usual excitement in antique shopping wasn't there. In the motel that night, I felt impending doom. On the way home the next day, dark clouds matched my mood. Forced to take a two-hour detour, I told Jack, "This entire trip has gone wrong." But the sun burst out during the beautifully scenic route, relieving my depression. A great peace filled me, as if God reached down and touched me. "I don't know why I had such a feeling of gloom," I told Jack.

When we arrived home, I found out why. Two of our girls came running from the house, their faces twisted in grief. Before I could get out of the car, the oldest flew into Jack's arms and cried, "Oh, Daddy, Grandma's dead!" My mother had lain dead for two days, all attempts to reach us having failed. Shocked and horrified, I wept. The pretty pink porcelain thimble with a heart proclaiming, "A mother is love," purchased as a gift for Mom, was now a reminder of grief. The meetings are, too.

I had no desire to attend last September's meeting. I thought it should be canceled, but the president decided to go ahead with it. I wanted to miss, but Jack encouraged me to go. On our return, as we drove into the driveway, I recalled the awful shock and horror of February. I realized then that my reticence involved much more than New York's tragedy. Subconsciously, I relived my own tragedy.

I will never forget the display of patriotism we witnessed on the way to Pennsylvania last September. This past weekend, I didn't see as many flags and patriotic signs. "How easily we forget," I thought. But I couldn't forget. I kept worrying about the kids. "Why are you worrying," Jack asked, "They'll be fine."

"How can we be sure?" I replied. But he was right. At home, my oldest daughter was there for me again, she and her sixteen-year-old son arriving ten minutes after us. They stayed the night and attended Sunday School. During the service, she renewed her covenant with God and my grandson accepted Christ as his Savior.

Sometimes we get a double whammy. I did last year. I did again this February 24th, but this time, good ones. One other girl was saved along with my grandson, and a young boy from our church had rededicated his life to God while I was gone. Life isn't all sunshine. But when dark clouds hover, the Son chases them away. Sunday morning, I could say with the Psalmist David, "*Return unto thy rest, O my soul, for the Lord hath dealt bountifully with thee.*" Psalm 116: 7 KJV

Printed in *The Jackson Herald*, March 6, 2002

GOD IS A DEMOLITION EXPERT

In our human imperfection, we are in need of a demolition expert, One who knows how to tear out inferior building materials while salvaging the good.

Two Powerful Tools: Prayer and Praise

"And at midnight Paul and Silas prayed, and sang praises unto God: and the prisoners heard them. And suddenly there was a great earthquake, so that the foundations of the prison were shaken: and immediately all the doors were opened, and everyone's bands were loosed." Acts 16: 25 & 26 KJV

I wonder what would have happened to Paul and Silas, during their imprisonment, if they had murmured and complained, if they had lost faith in God's providence? But these faithful men taught us two great lessons: God dwells in praise; Satan flees from it.

Sometimes we Christians find ourselves, like Paul and Silas, bound by chains. Not literal shackles, but constricting and disabling bands of doubt or discouragement.

In the midst of spiritual imprisonment, if we pray and lift our hands and voices in praise to God, as Paul and Silas did, these two actions will shake our foundation of fear, tear down walls of spiritual weariness, and open up doors we can walk through. Prayer and praise loosen chains of bondage and set us free.

Sometime changes in our situation or mindset aren't immediate. Sometimes the walls are slow in coming down. My father, before his retirement and death, owned a demolition business. He didn't use either dynamite or a wrecking ball to immediately bring a structure down, but piece by piece, with great care, he dismantled those walls, salvaging goods.

94

Sometimes God slowly tears down walls that separate us from Him, in order to salvage something precious and beautiful. We learn and grow in the process. We store in our minds and hearts materials from the experience with which to rebuild a marriage, a life, or a lasting relationship with Him.

My father kept good building materials and destroyed the rotted and broken boards. God eliminates defective characteristics and defeating habits in our Christian lives and builds for us from the salvageable materials a safe dwelling place. Trust in God doesn't assure us peace in this world (although it does assure us of peace in our hearts, if we remain in His love), but if we allow Him to construct for us a strong spiritual house, winds of adversity won't bring down our sturdy walls of faith.

Trials, like an earthquake, may shake our spirituality, but our foundation will remain strong and unmovable. Floods of fear may sometimes overflow, chilling and frightening, but they will eventually pass, leaving us stronger in the aftermath.

Our pastor once preached about how winds of adversity may blow Christians this way and that but not move them from the Foundation. I thought of the segmented little plastic toys fastened to a small round box. Pushing up at different locations on the movable bottom of the box causes the little creatures to flop this way and that, sometimes bend over backwards or fall to their knees. But the feet, anchored firm, never move out of place.

That's the way Christians should be. We should plant our feet firmly on the Rock, bend over backwards to avoid animosity with others, and stay on our knees in prayer. When trials come, and Satan pushes us around, chin up and knees down should be our reaction.

Printed in *The Jackson Herald*, March 20, 2002

EVEN UNTO OLD AGE, WE FIGHT OUR BATTLES

Soldier of Misfortune

In February of 1945, during World War II, a young man named Frank Miller, Senior, left home to answer Uncle Sam's call to support his country. Three small children and a wife mourned his leaving. I was the youngest of those children. Four at the time, I have no memory of my father's departure, only vague memories of occurrences during his absence.

I recall my mother and I holding hands on a warm, sunny afternoon, laughing and happy as we made our way to join my brother and sister in the school's annual egghunt. I remember scouring a hillside for brightly colored eggs and returning to the little one-room schoolhouse with my Easter basket full.

I remember my brother and sister's vehement yells and the sound of their fists banging on the door of our landlord's woodshed when he mischievously locked them in. I recall the awful fear and betrayal I felt, not old enough to understand the prank and my mother's laughter.

I remember Mom sitting in a chair, laughing as we blew bubble gum into huge bubbles, then teaching us a lesson on manners as we popped those bubbles on her bare knee.

I recall standing in a warm spring rain on the porch of our little rented home, watching in awe as huge raindrops, splashing in king's crowns off the concrete, appeared to turn into miniature, hopping toads. Mom told us that the toads were sucked up in dry weather as frog eggs and fell from the sky with the rain.

I have never forgotten the joy of receiving the colorful wool weaving, lace-edged silk hankie, and the sparkling blue ring from my father, shipped to me before he was shipped overseas from Hawaii on the Peugeot Sound. But I have also not forgotten my anxiety as we searched our postage-stamp lawn for my lost ring, my sorrow and guilt when it was never found. I still have the hanky and scarf in my cedar chest.

But my loss was forgotten, my guilt relieved, when we met my father at the train station in November, 1945, welcoming him home after ten months of missing him. The war had ended in September as his ship sailed across the ocean. Not realizing the blessing in this timing didn't lessen my excitement while waiting in the train station, watching a mammoth engine puff out clouds of black cinders and white-suited men pouring from open doors of passenger cars.

Finding each other in the crush, Mom and Dad kissed. Dad's eyes, the color of spring bluetts, shone with tears as he whirled Mom around in a happy waltz, then plunked his jaunty white Navy cap down over my brother's ears. My loss was not all that seemed forgotten when he offered my brother and sister a piece of chewing gum. My mother smiled and nodded toward me. "Nancy's old enough to chew gum now, " she said.

A photo of my proud father in dark-blue Navy dress, displayed in my living room, reminds me of those bittersweet days. My father's absence in 1945 was forced. His absence in 2000 at the age of eighty-six was voluntary. But the memory of this later absence is not blurred, as the first, but indelible on my mind and heart.

Suffering with Alzheimer's, Dad walked away from home, clad only in light workshirt and pants, on a bitterly cold October evening that year, in spite of Mom's efforts to restrain him. This time, there was no happy return. Four months later, Mom died of a massive heart attack, alone in her backyard, perhaps grieving herself to death.

There were no happy memories during Dad's absence, only worry, despair and sleepless nights. My heartache and guilt over the loss of my ring that long ago day couldn't compare to the deep heartache and guilt I now experienced. Why weren't we more insistent that Mom and Dad not live alone? But, like my brother and sister locked in that frightening woodshed, we were prisoners of Mom's stubbornness, beating our heads against a brick wall in trying to convince her they needed help.

In April of 2001, my father's body was discovered, caught under a barbed wire fence and covered with a blanket of leaves. As I observed veterans of war giving my father a military fifteen-gun salute at his funeral, I wondered how many of the older men may have served in World War II, how many might succumb to the same disease that stole my father's faculties and took his life.

I didn't know how to express my gratitude to these men for serving my country and paying allegiance to my father, but my youngest grandson, four at the time, knew just what to do. Walking up to an elderly veteran, he stood for a solemn moment with his head lifted, gazing into the man's eyes, then lifted his little hand in a smart salute. I could hear Dad's prophecy when he first held this newborn grandson: "There's a spirit about this boy. I believe he will become a great man of God."

It's too soon to tell about my grandson Stone, but that sailor of long ago did become a great man of God. When he had forgotten how to garden, Dad could still stand in church and praise God, quoting the Twenty-third Psalm. When he had forgotten my name or that I was his daughter, he could still sing, "Just a Closer Walk with Thee."

My ring may be lost forever, but my father is not. On the night Dad walked away, God gave me a scripture to read just before I learned of his disappearance. Psalm 71 asks God to not let us be put to confusion. It speaks of how God will not

98

cast us off in old age, of how He will not forsake us when our strength fails.

Verse 20 reads: "*Thou, which has shewed me great and sore troubles, shalt quicken me again, and shalt bring me up again from the depths of the earth.*" I later imagined God's angel tenderly reaching down, lifting Dad from his deathbed of autumn leaves, and winging him off to glory, where his confusion and war with senility ended.

Verses 22 and 23 of the Seventy-first Psalm continue: "*I will also praise thee with the psaltery, even thy truth, O my God: unto thee will I sing with the harp, O thou Holy One of Israel. My lips shall greatly rejoice when I sing unto thee.*" At the funeral, I could hear Dad praising God, singing as he walked with Jesus, "Just a Closer Walk with Thee."

Dad, I still have the hanky and beautiful scarf you gave me. I wish I hadn't lost the ring. But, most of all, I wish I hadn't lost you. I salute you, Dad, for your faithful service to God and country. I will try to serve my Savior as valiantly as you served Him, so that one day we can once again reunite with happy tears.

A family reunited after Dad's happy homecoming from World War II. Back row: Mom and Dad. Front row, left to right: me, my only brother, Frank, Junior ("Bub"), and my oldest sister, Eleanor Roberta Louise ("Doodie").

Handsome and proud, Dad poses in front of navy barracks
after his induction into the United States Navy

CARING CORRESPONDENCE

So many sent cards, letters, and e-mails during our tragedy. A good friend of mine wrote the following poem before Dad was found. It so aptly expressed the way we felt in those trying months about his destiny.

For Nancy's Dad

He walked away one fine fall day;
where he was going he didn't say.
All who love him just wait and pray,
and still – yet still – he's missing.

This gray and aged, unwell man,
this one so kind through all life's span,
one bent by time's cruel, calloused hand,
walked away – walked away –still missing.

Family, friends, and searchers all,
through woods, over hills you heard their call.
So many places he could fall.
Hour by hour and day by day – still, he's missing.

Oh, God, You know, You understand.
You hold his fate and soul in hand.
His loved ones know and understand,
And to You, God, and You alone – he's not missing.

_ Carolyn H. Brown

Thanks, Carolyn

"I Will Wait, Till My Change Come"
Job: 14:14

As autumn leaves blaze their glory,
Then fade and die and fall from trees,
I find my life, in seasons' rushing,
Fades more quickly than I please.
It seems but just a tear, some laughter,
A bit of sadness, a moment's joy,
Like vapor drawn by distant sun,
And soon, too soon, life is over.
O, God Eternal, forever living
In death's realm where I am drawn,
Will my life, like earth's vapor,
Dissipate and then be done?
Or, as earth's unclean waters,
Purified by heaven's heat,
Will I come, my soul cleansed,
To bow, perfected, at your feet?
Is the change mere transformation,
As the vapor becomes rain.
And having drawn me to your bosom,
Will you renew this life again?
Will I run in your vast kingdom
As the child I used to be,
Regain the innocence and wonder,
Now jaded by reality?
Then shine, O Son, more intently,
Your lovelight's warmth drawing me
From this vale of disillusion,
Lift me gently, Lord to thee.

Mom and Dad, I'm glad your trials and tragedies are past. We miss you terribly, but we can now rest assured that you are both safe in the Father's keeping. As your souls soared high above the earth, your destination heaven, your mature seeds of love wafted back to us on the gentle breath of time, lodging in our hearts and blossoming into fragrant, golden remembrances and sunny thoughts, drawing us closer to the heart of God.

My Family-1987

Left to Right: Frank ("Bub") Miller, Junior, Eleanor Roberta Louise ("Doodie") McFadden, Mom, Dad, Sheila Ann Byrne, born soon after Dad's return from the Navy, and Deborah Kay Vanbibber, born nine years after Sheila.

DEATH AWAITS US ALL

Although you may not die as tragic a death as my mother and father, rest assured, death will come, with no avenue of escape. Life on this earth is fleeting, as a vapor that soon vanishes away. I pray that through the reading of this book, those of you not prepared for the finality of death and the hereafter will make preparations for your final journey.

Suffering does not begin and end with the human race. God suffered the death of a loved one, but, unlike us, He chose to suffer, in order to redeem mankind.

"For God so loved the world, that he gave his only begotten Son, that whosoever believeth in him should not perish, but have everlasting life." John 3:16 KJV

As God comforts us in our suffering, we should seek to comfort others.

"Blessed be God, even the Father of our Lord Jesus Christ, the Father of mercies, and the God of all comfort: Who comforteth us in all our tribulation, that we may be able to comfort them which are in any trouble, by the comfort wherewith we ourselves are comforted of God."
II Corinthians 1:3 & 4 KJV

I pray that the reading of this book will bring a measure of comfort to sufferers and instill a full knowledge of Christ into hurting and seeking hearts.

Back cover author's photo: Wanda Hartley Butts